THE HEALTHY KITCHEN

JUICES & SMOOTHIES

hinkler

CONTENTS

Introduction	3
Superfoods	7
Fruits and Vegetables	25
Energy Boosters	43
Healing Elixirs	61
Healthy Gourmet	79
Weights and Measures	94
Index	96

hinkler

Published by Hinkler Books Pty Ltd
45–55 Fairchild Street
Heatherton Victoria 3202 Australia
www.hinkler.com.au

Design © Hinkler Books Pty Ltd 2015, 2016
Food photography and recipe development
© Stockfood, The Food Media Agency
Typesetting: MPS Limited
Prepress: Graphic Print Group

All rights reserved. No part of this publication may be reproduced, stored in a retrieval system, or transmitted in any way or by any means, electronic, mechanical, photocopying, recording or otherwise, without the prior written permission of Hinkler Books Pty Ltd.

ISBN: 978 1 4889 3004 1

Printed and bound in China

JUICES AND SMOOTHIES

Drinking juices and smoothies is an easy, healthy way to increase the amount of essential vitamins, minerals, nutrients and fibre in your diet. Just a few minutes of preparation and machine set-up is all it takes to create delicious and nutritious drinks. Incorporating the recommended quantity of fruits and vegetables per day has never been easier, and preparing juices and smoothies makes it simple to introduce a diverse range of fruits and vegetables to your diet that might otherwise be hard to consume.

Incorporating Juices and Smoothies into a Healthy Diet

While freshly pressed juices and smoothies are undoubtedly beneficial, they should not be a replacement for a healthy, balanced diet. Add them as a supplement to a wholesome, varied diet combined with plenty of exercise. To fully harness the health benefits of these drinks, don't simply drink the same juices and smoothies every week; instead, alternate the recipes so that you get a good mix of different vitamins, minerals and other nutrients over the course of a few weeks.

When selecting produce, try to add dark, leafy green vegetables to your juice and smoothie recipes, as well as nutrient-dense vegetables such as beetroot (beet), carrot and avocado. Fruits such as bananas and grapes should be used in moderation to help control the impact of high amounts of fructose. After drinking juices or smoothies containing fruit, rinse your mouth with water and avoid brushing your teeth straight away to prevent damage to your teeth enamel.

If you need to restrict your fruit intake for health reasons, vegetable juices and smoothies are an excellent option. For kids who are reluctant to eat vegetables, juices and smoothies are a fun way to ensure they still get the health benefits vegetables offer.

Some recipes in this book include a small amount of sugar for taste. If you have concerns about adding sugar or need to limit your sugar intake, the amount of sugar can be reduced, the sugar can be left out altogether or a sugar substitute could be used. The same applies to other sweet ingredients such as honey.

Try to source and use organic produce where possible. Organic produce is certified to be free of pesticides and preservatives that may alter the flavour of your drinks as well as their nutritional benefits.

Using these Recipes

If you are not used to drinking juices or smoothies, or you're using juices and smoothies to kickstart a change in your dietary habits, begin with common fruits and vegetables that you enjoy eating. Mild-flavoured fruits and vegetables, such as apples, carrots and watermelons, are good ingredients to begin with as they are easy on the stomach.

As your body adjusts to your increased intake of vitamins, minerals and nutrients, you can begin to introduce more variety, as well as fruits and vegetables you may not be used to eating. You can introduce beetroot for its cleansing properties, and nutrient-rich green vegetables such as celery, kale and spinach. Then you can begin to make juices and smoothies with more exotic or unusual ingredients, and even experiment with your own healthy combinations!

What to Add to Juices and Smoothies

Smoothies are an easy way to top up your protein intake; a 30 g serve of whey protein powder can contain around 25 g of protein. For those with dietary needs or restrictions, protein powders are readily available in varieties such as soy, casein and even plant-based types.

For an added boost of healthy fats, you can try adding chia, flax or hemp seeds to your next smoothie. These seeds contain essential amino acids, omega-3 and antioxidants, as well as having anti-inflammatory properties.

Additional supplements such as spirulina powder can be added to fresh vegetable juices; a little agave nectar or organic honey helps with reducing the distinctive flavour.

A Note for Vegans

All of the recipes in this book are suitable for vegetarians and many of them are also suitable for vegans. Those recipes that use animal products can easily be adapted for vegans. For example, you can use soy, almond or coconut milk in place or normal milk, and dairy yoghurt can be replaced with soy or rice yoghurt which are becoming more readily available. Maple or rice syrup can be used in place of honey, and egg replacements can be used in place of eggs.

Equipment

When it comes to selecting equipment, blenders with a powerful motor are able to break down fruits and softer vegetables to a smoother consistency. For best results, look for blenders with at least 600W of power that use angled or bent blades. For harder vegetables, you will want to use a dedicated juicer that will remove some of the insoluble fibre but also extract the most juice from your produce.

Proper care of a good blender or juicer will prolong its useful life. To clean a blender, it's best to wash it with warm soapy water. Half fill your blender with warm water and then add half a teaspoon of liquid soap. Replace the lid of the blender and then run it on a medium setting for 10–15 seconds to help wash out the inside and the blades. Drain, rinse with warm water, and then pat dry with paper towels, paying particular attention to the blades to help prevent rusting. To clean a juicer, dismantle and rinse the parts under running water. Clean the strainer with an old toothbrush. Then wash with a mild detergent and rinse well.

Consuming and Storing Your Juices and Smoothies

Once exposed to air, natural ingredients such as fruit and vegetables begin to lose their nutrients and spoil, so whether you make a cleansing juice or a nutrition-packed smoothie, enjoy it straight away for best results!

If you do need to store your juice or smoothie, carefully pour it into an airtight thermos or glass jar. Avoid leaving space at the top to prevent oxidisation. Wrap glass jars in foil to stop light from affecting the enzymes. Keep your juice or smoothie in the refrigerator for no more than one day.

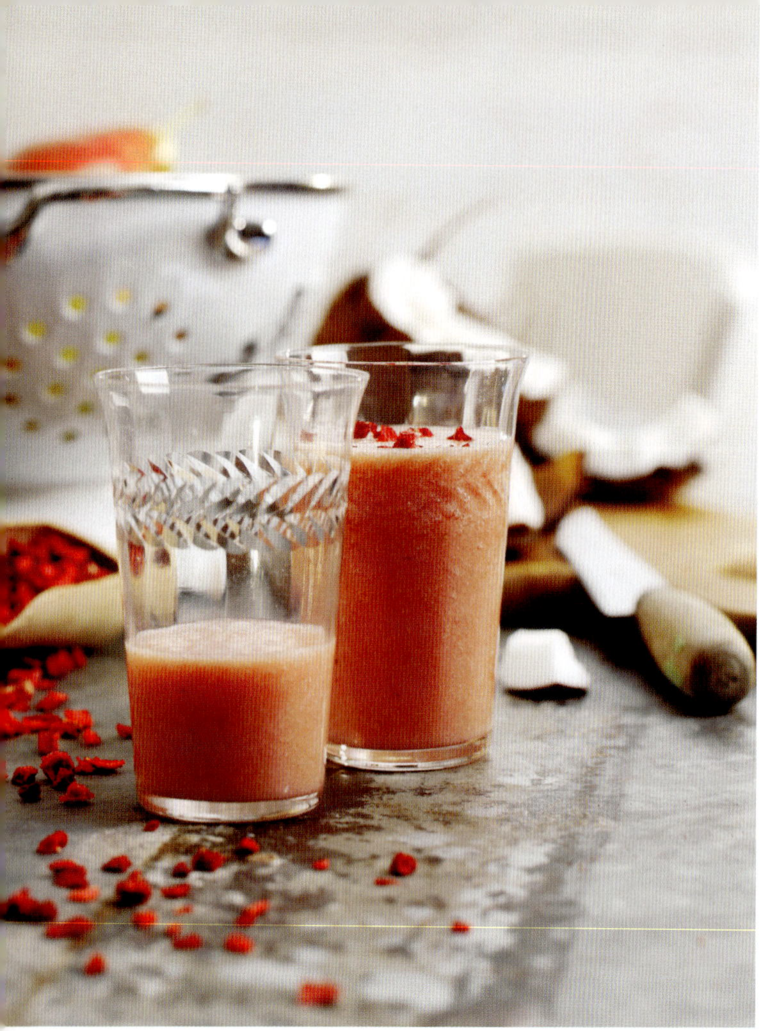
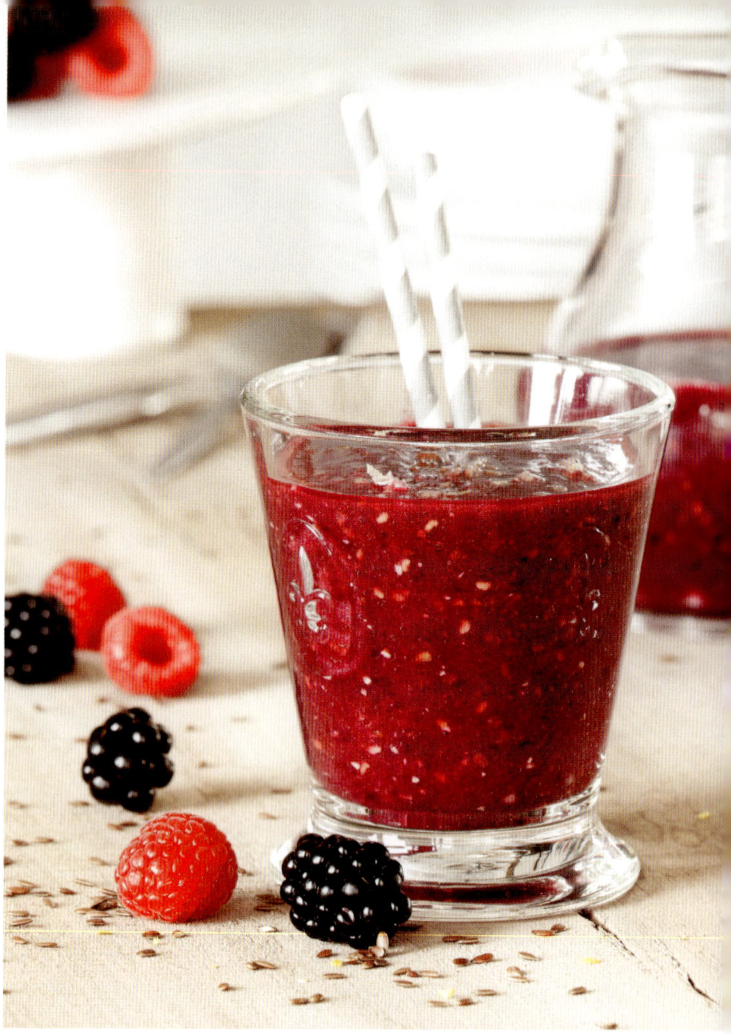
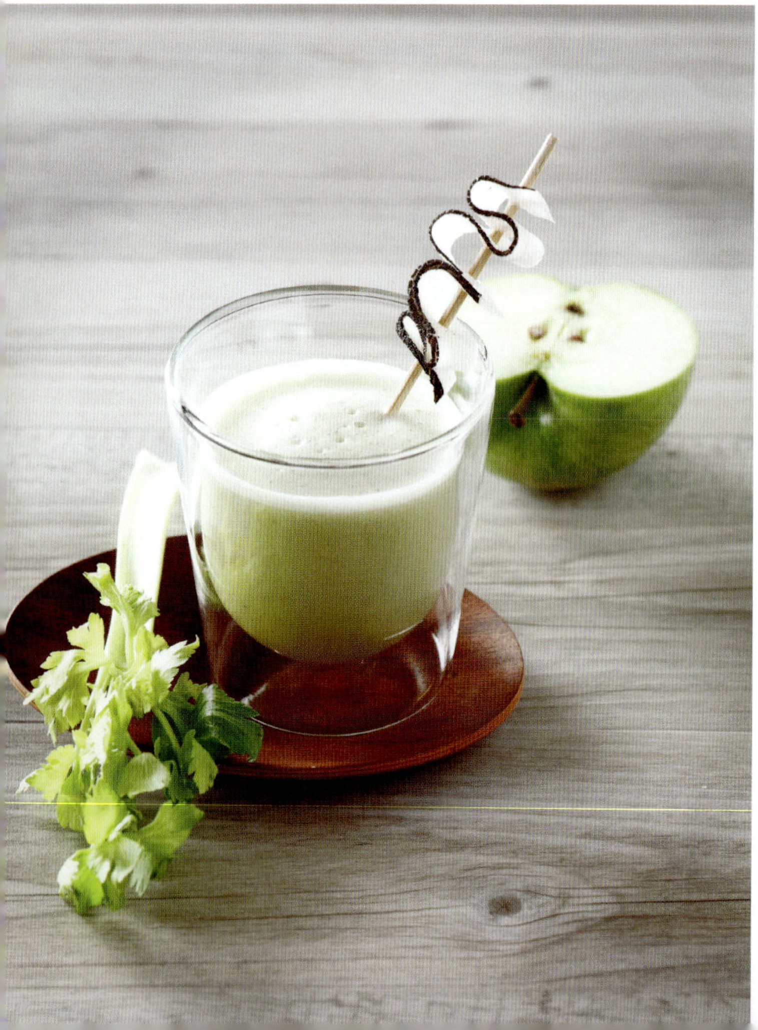
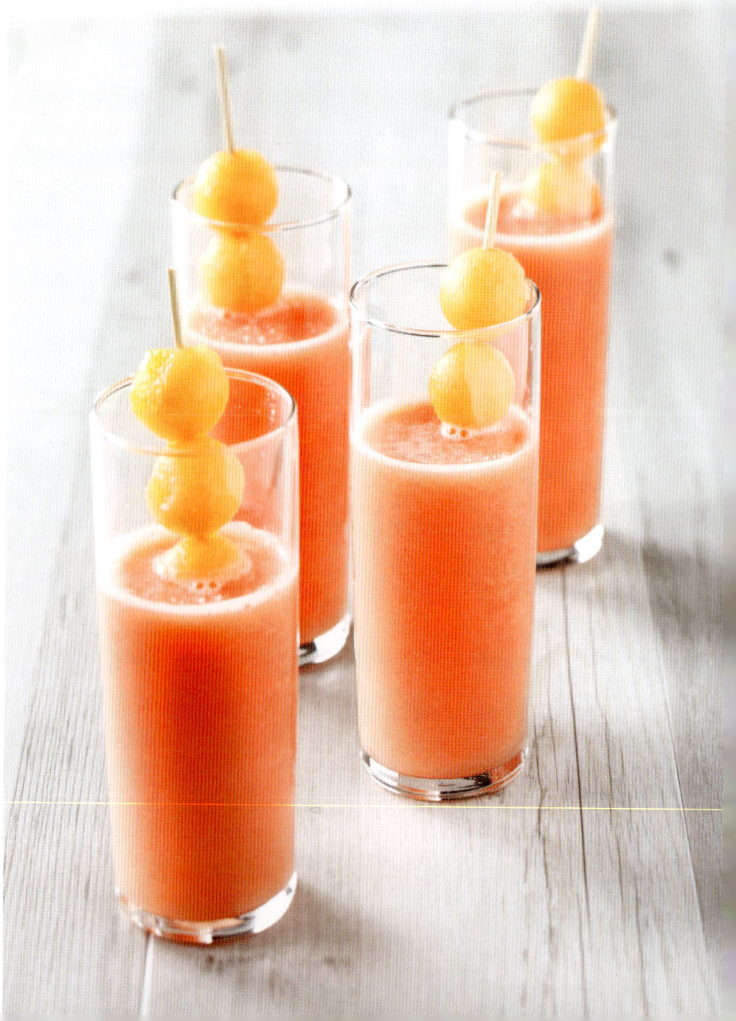

SUPERFOODS

Nutrient-dense superfoods can help bolster your health, but incorporating them into your diet can be challenging. Packed with ingredients such as berries, spinach, chia seeds and kumquats, these juice and smoothie recipes are a terrific way to enjoy some food superstars!

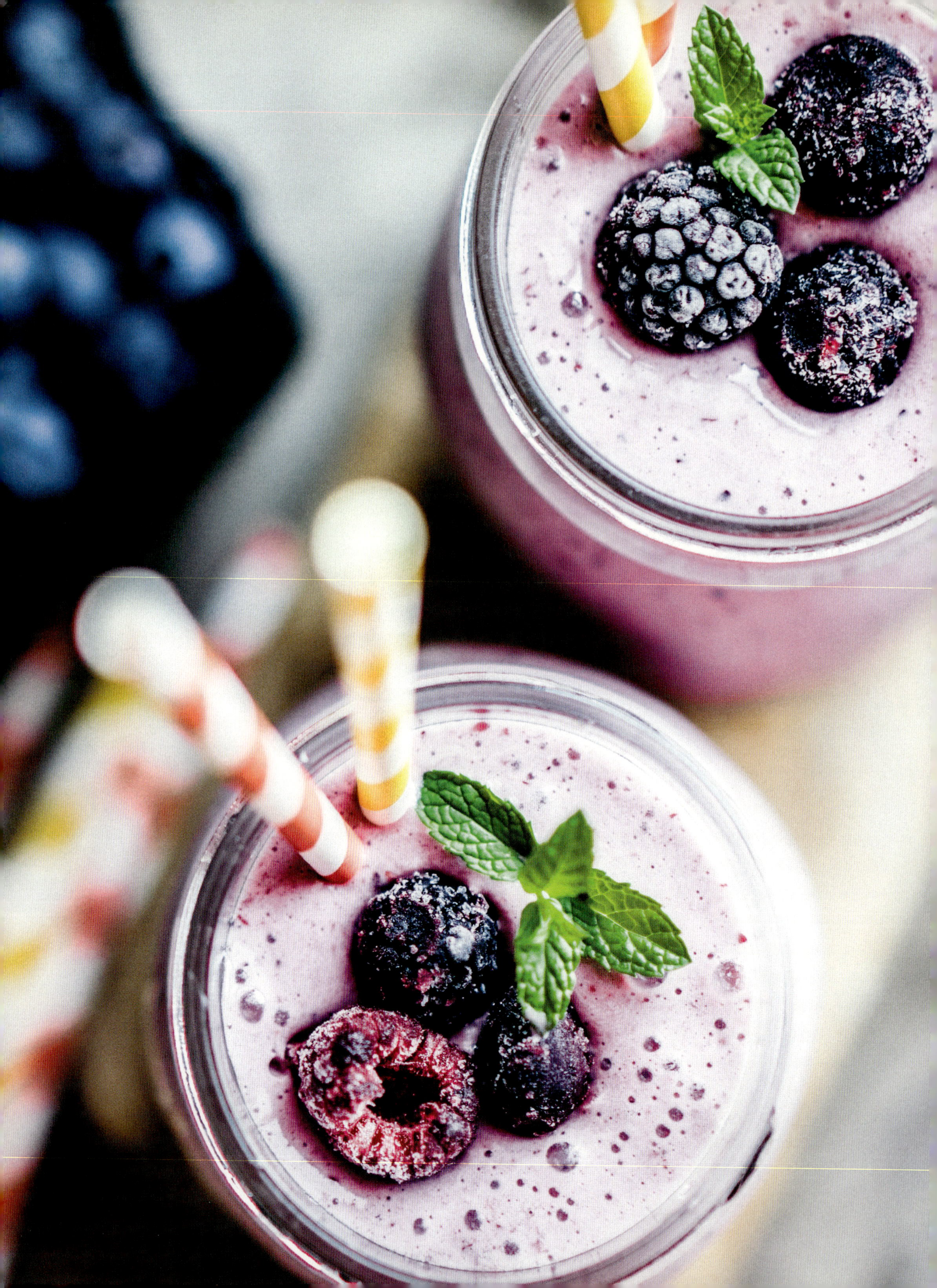

BERRY SMOOTHIES

Serves 2
Preparation 3 minutes

Ingredients:

150 g | 5 oz | 1 cup frozen blueberries
150 g | 5 oz | 1 cup frozen blackberries
400 ml | 14 fl oz | 1⅔ cups coconut milk
2 tsp acai berry powder
2 tbsp runny honey
2 sprigs mint

Method:

1. Reserve four blueberries and two blackberries for the garnish and put the rest of the berries in a blender.

2. Add the coconut milk, acai powder and honey and blend until smooth.

3. Pour into two glasses, top with mint sprigs and the reserved berries and serve immediately.

STRAWBERRY AND COCONUT SMOOTHIES WITH GOJI BERRIES

Serves 2
Preparation and cooking 7 minutes

Ingredients:

2 tbsp goji berries, plus extra to garnish
150 g | 5 oz | 1 cup frozen strawberries
1 ripe pear, peeled, cored and diced
300 ml | 11 fl oz | 1⅓ cups coconut water

Method:

1. Put the goji berries in a small bowl and cover with boiling water. Leave to soften for 5 minutes, then drain well.

2. Put the goji berries in a blender with the strawberries, pear and coconut water and blend until smooth. Divide between two small glasses and serve sprinkled with a few more goji berries.

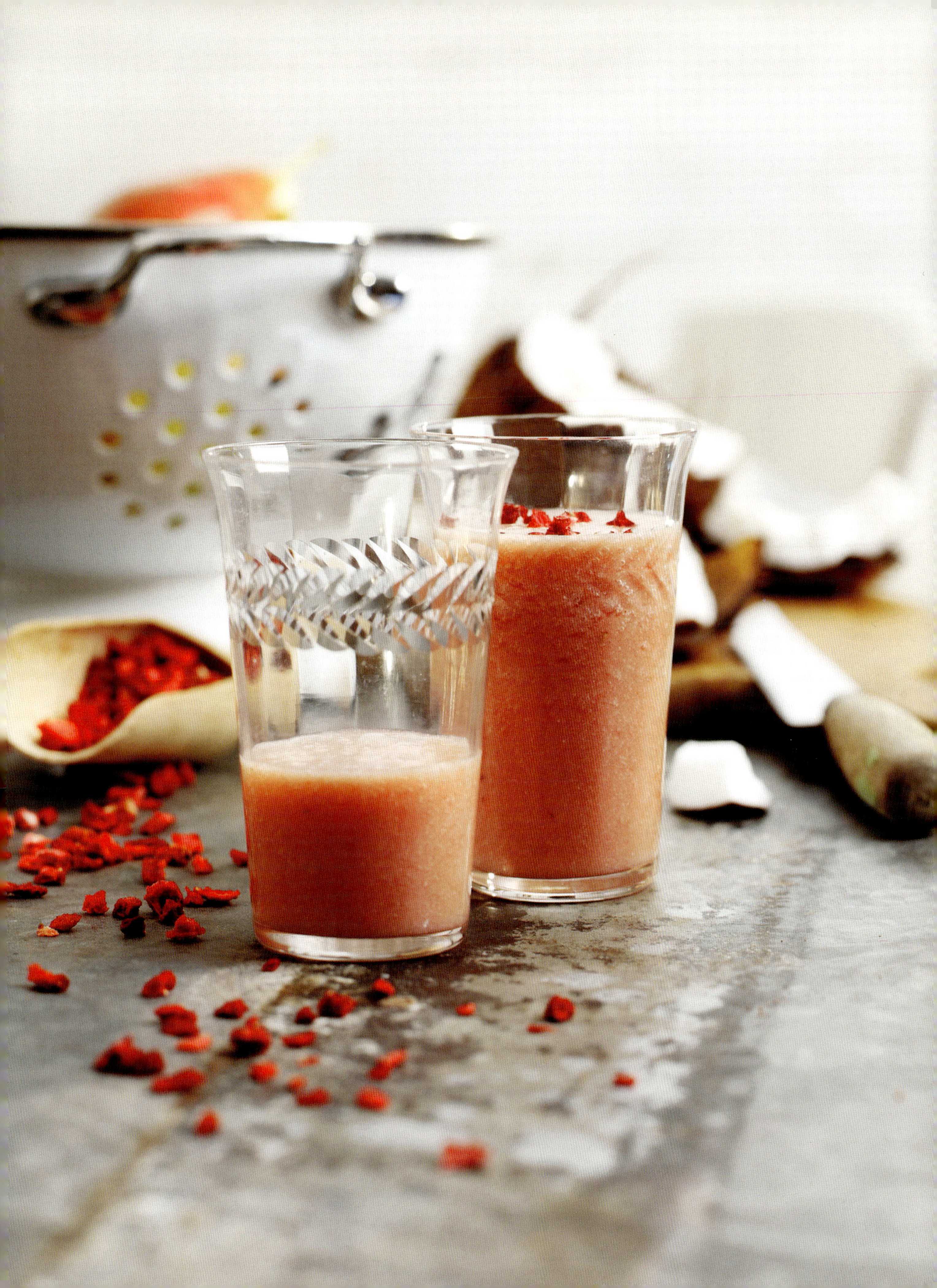

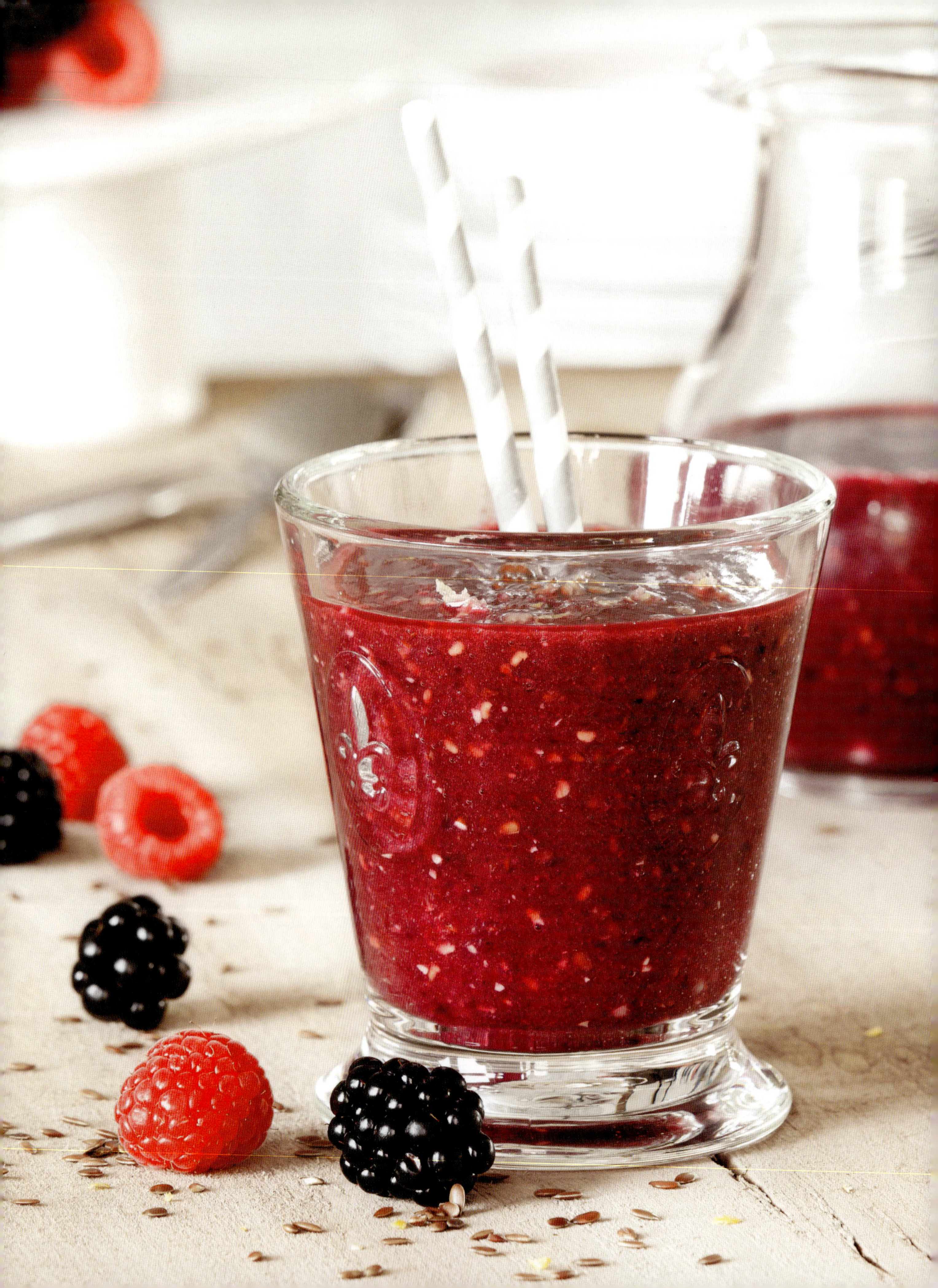

BLACKBERRY AND RASPBERRY SMOOTHIES

Serves 4
Preparation 10 minutes

Ingredients:

300 g | 11 oz | 2 cups frozen raspberries
200 g | 7 oz | 1⅓ cups blackberries
150 g | 5 oz | ⅔ cup vanilla yoghurt
250 ml | 9 fl oz | 1 cup semi-skimmed milk
1 tbsp light agave nectar
250 g | 9 oz | 1 cup crushed ice

Method:

1. Combine the raspberries, blackberries, yoghurt, milk and agave nectar in a food blender or processor.

2. Blend until smooth. Add the crushed ice and blend again until smooth.

3. Pour into glasses and serve with straws.

Tip: Add a handful of frozen blackcurrants or blueberries for a three-berry smoothie.

APPLE, CELERY AND BLACK RADISH JUICE

Serves 2
Preparation 6 minutes

Ingredients:

2 × 10 cm | 4 in black radishes (black mooli)
3 Granny Smith apples, quartered
4 stalks celery

Method:

1. Cut the radishes into quarters lengthways, then use a vegetable peeler to shave two thin ribbons. Thread each radish shaving onto a skewer and set aside for the garnish.

2. Put the rest of the radish through a juicer with the apple and celery, then stir well and serve with the radish garnish.

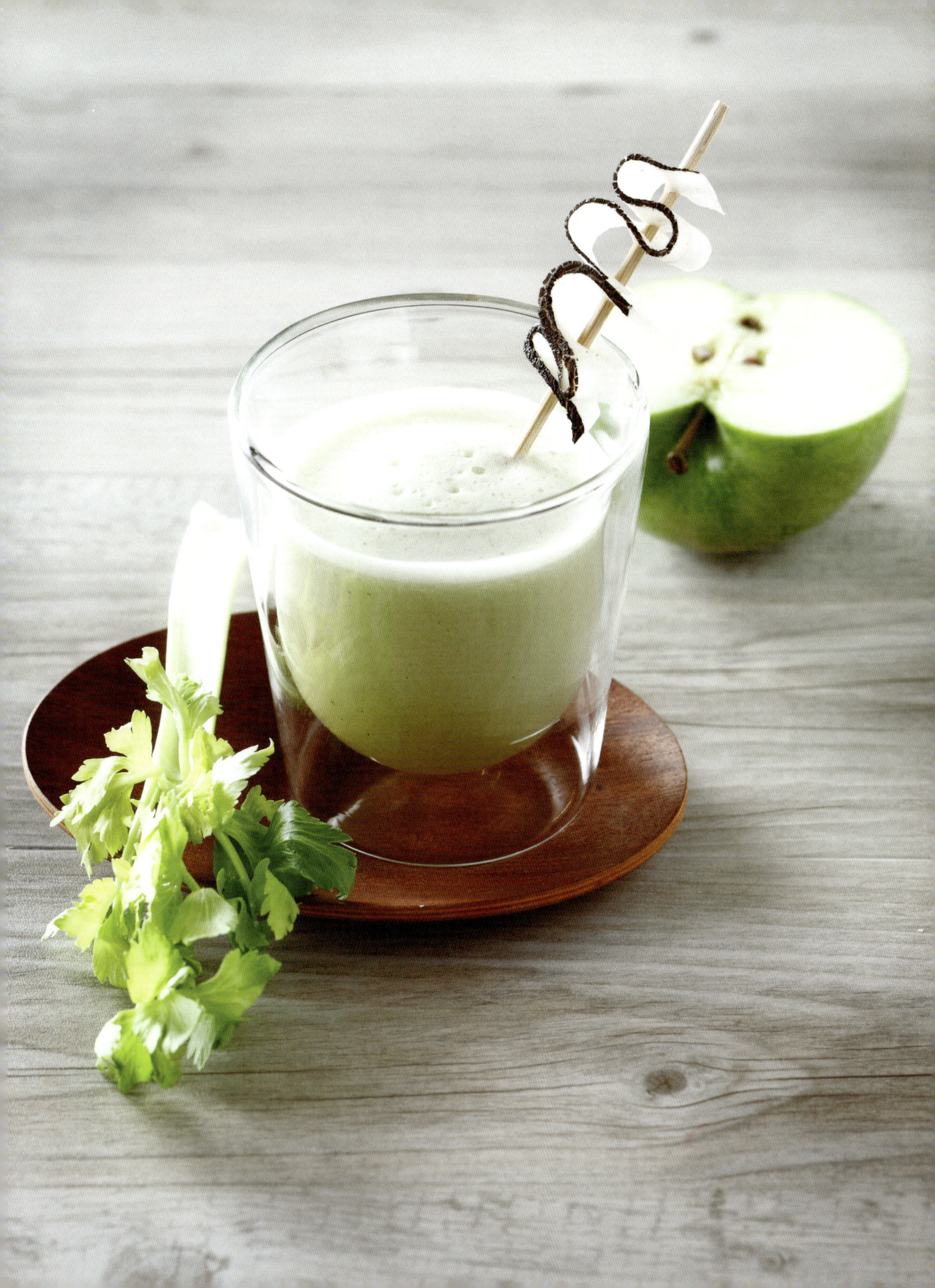

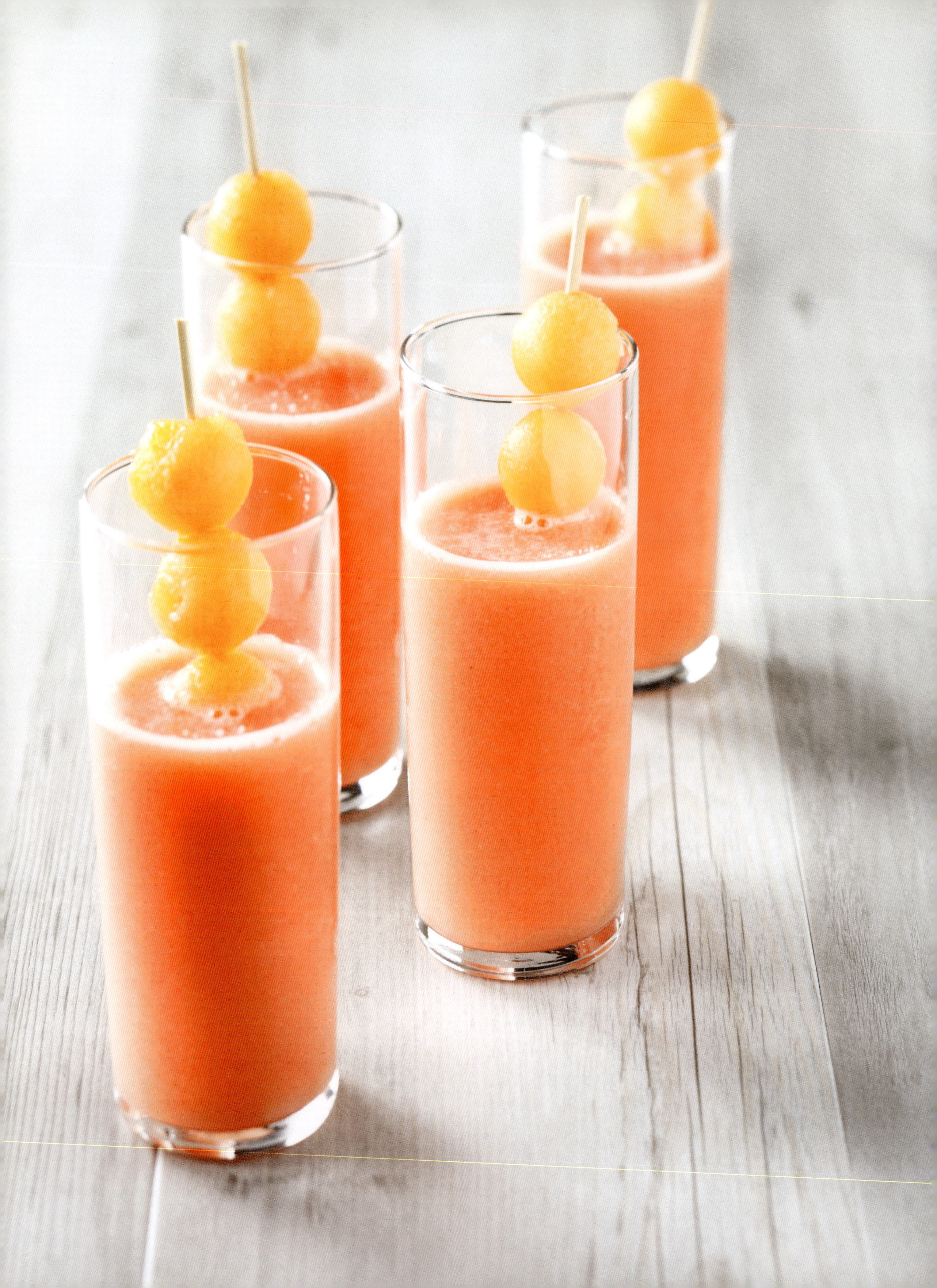

STRAWBERRY AND MELON ANTIOXIDANT JUICE

Serves 4
Preparation 6 minutes

Ingredients:

2 small rockmelons (cantaloupes), halved and seeds removed
200 g | 7 oz | 1⅓ cups strawberries

Method:

1. Use a melon-baller to make twelve melon balls and thread them onto four wooden skewers for the garnish.

2. Scoop the rest of the flesh from the melons and put it through a juicer with the strawberries.

3. Divide the juice between four glasses and add a melon skewer to each one.

KUMQUAT AND PINEAPPLE JUICE

Serves 4
Preparation 15 minutes

Ingredients:

1 small pineapple, peeled, cored and diced
300 g | 11 oz | 2 cups kumquats, peeled
250 ml | 9 fl oz | 1 cup orange juice
250 ml | 9 fl oz | 1 cup cold sparkling water
1 lime, cut into wedges
55 g | 2 oz | ⅔ cup desiccated (fine) coconut

Method:

1. Combine together the pineapple, kumquat flesh, orange juice and sparkling water in a food processor or blender.

2. Blend on high for 2 minutes until smooth. Rub the rims of four serving glasses with the lime wedges.

3. Dip the glasses in desiccated (fine) coconut to coat. Fill with the juice before serving.

Tip: Use chilled still water if sparkling is not available.

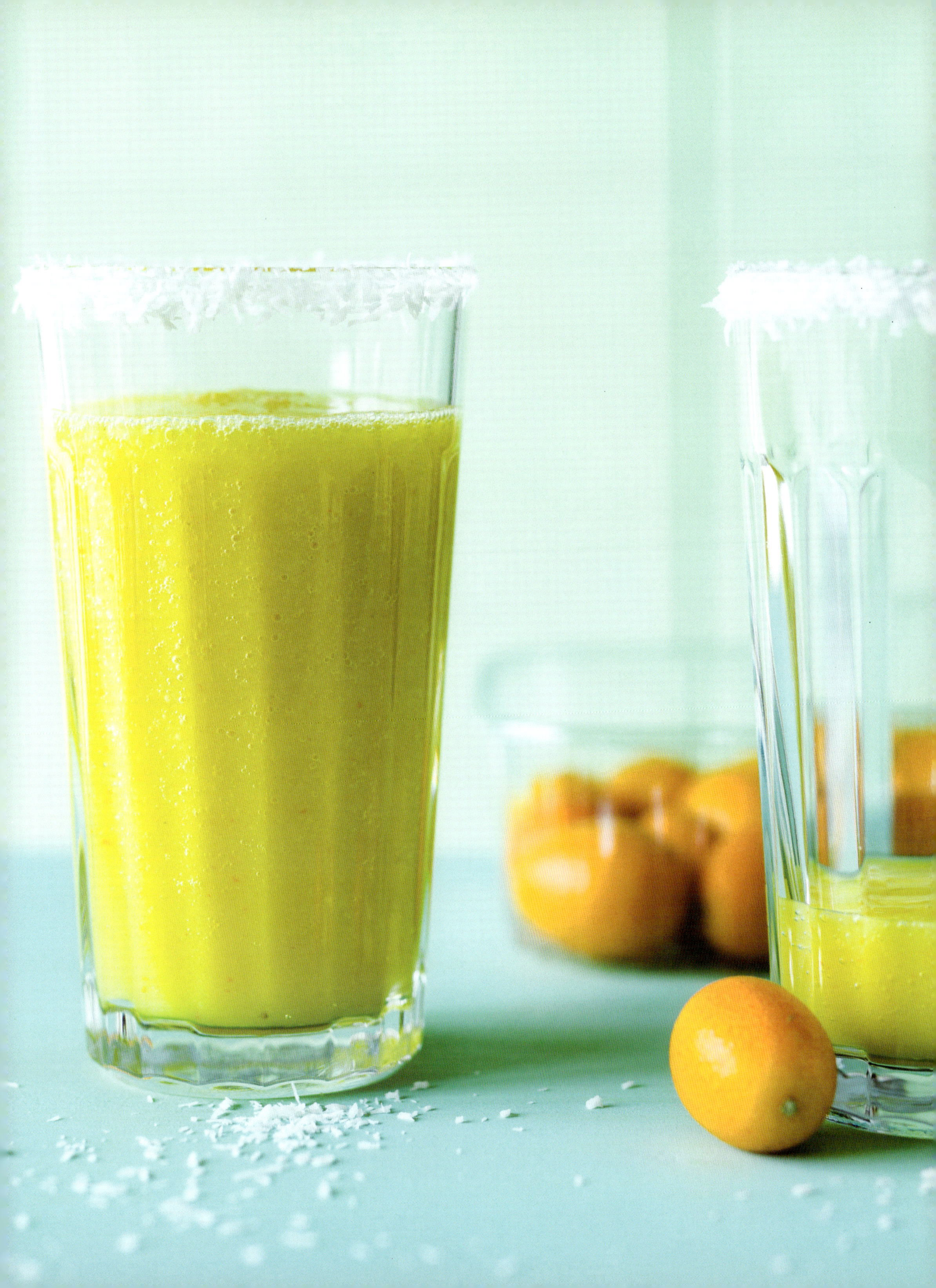

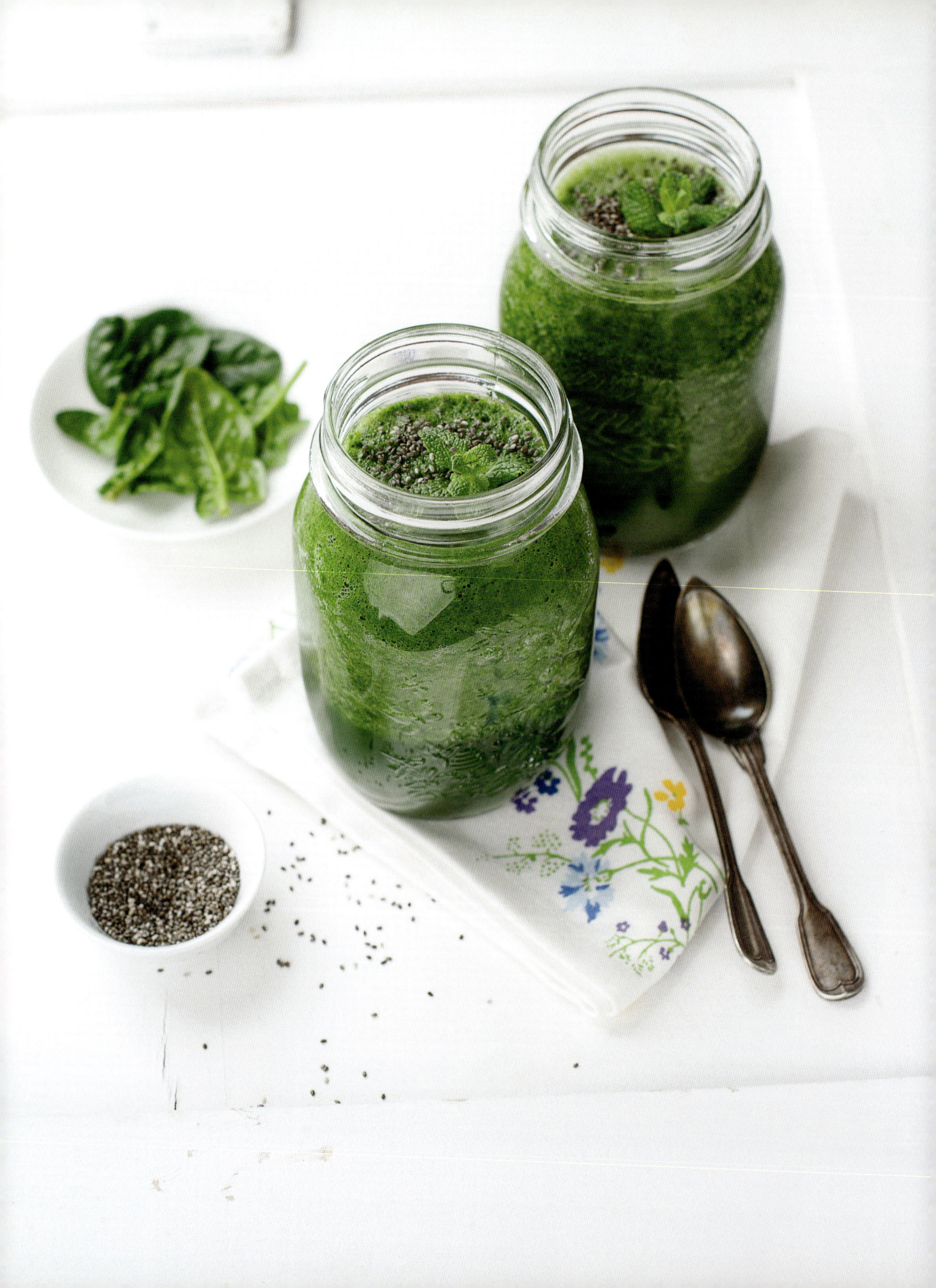

SPINACH AND PEAR SMOOTHIES WITH CHIA SEEDS

Serves 2
Preparation 5 minutes + freezing 2 hours

Ingredients:

2 ripe pears, peeled, cored and diced
35 g | 1¼ oz | 1 cup baby spinach
250 ml | 9 fl oz | 1 cup apple juice
1½ tbsp chia seeds, plus extra for sprinkling
6 sprigs mint

Method:

1. Spread the diced pears out on a lined baking tray (sheet) and freeze for 2 hours or until solid.

2. Put the spinach in a blender with the apple juice, chia seeds and four sprigs of mint. Blend until smooth.

3. Add the frozen pear to the blender and blend until smooth, then divide between two glasses. Top each one with a mint sprig and an extra sprinkle of chia seeds.

VITAMIN-RICH JUICE

Serves 4
Preparation 10 minutes

Ingredients:

800 g | 28 oz pineapple, sliced
1 small beetroot (beet), peeled and chopped
2-3 carrots, chopped

Method:

1. Put all the ingredients into a juicer and blend until smooth. Chill.

2. Pour into chilled serving glasses.

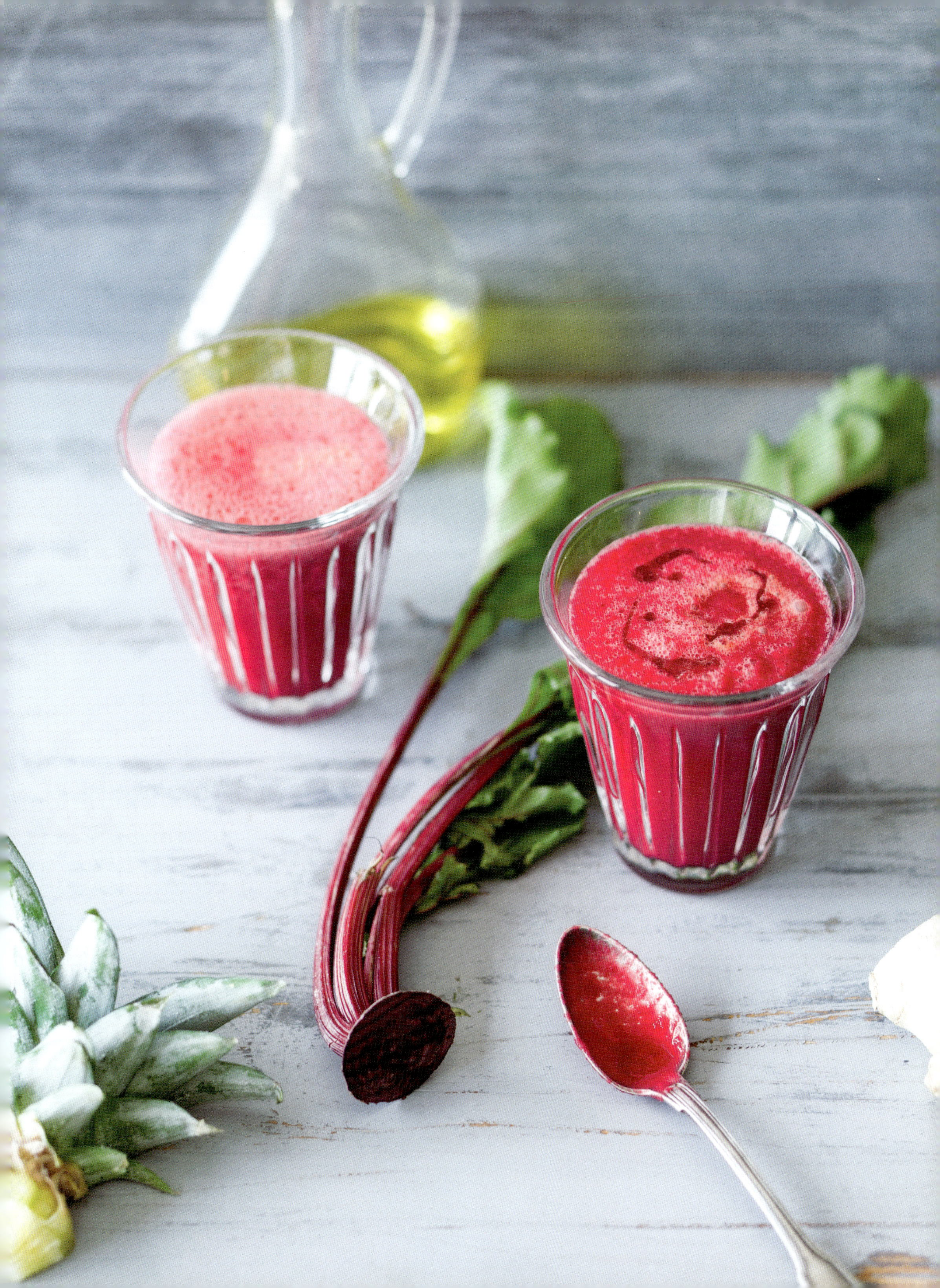

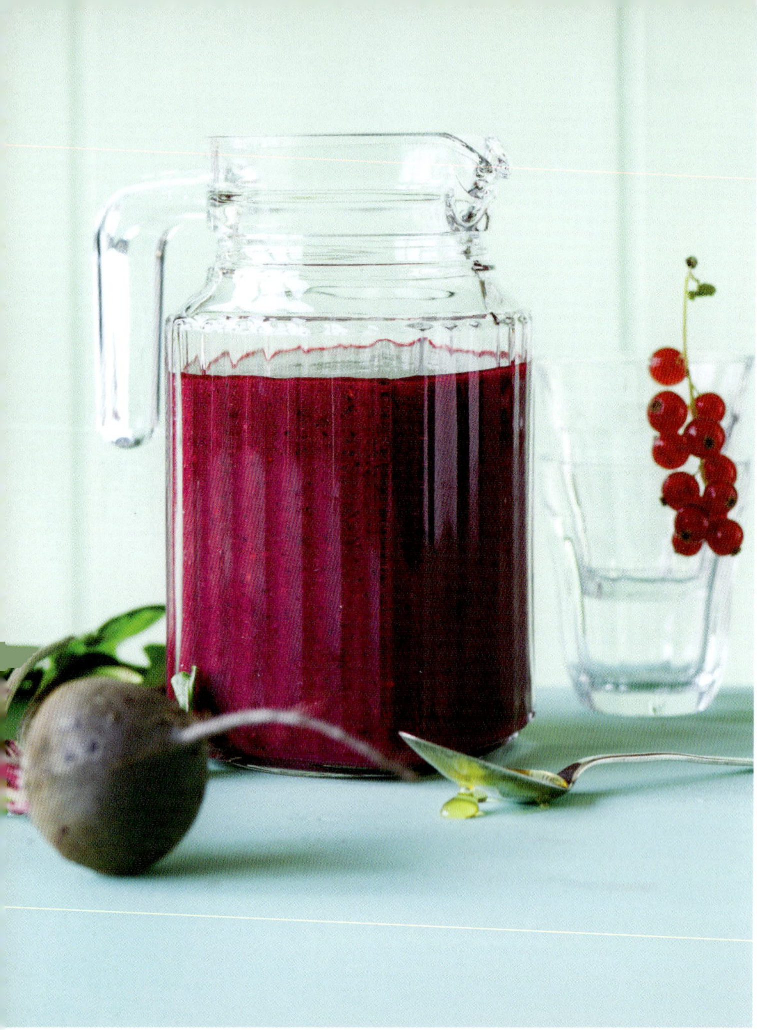

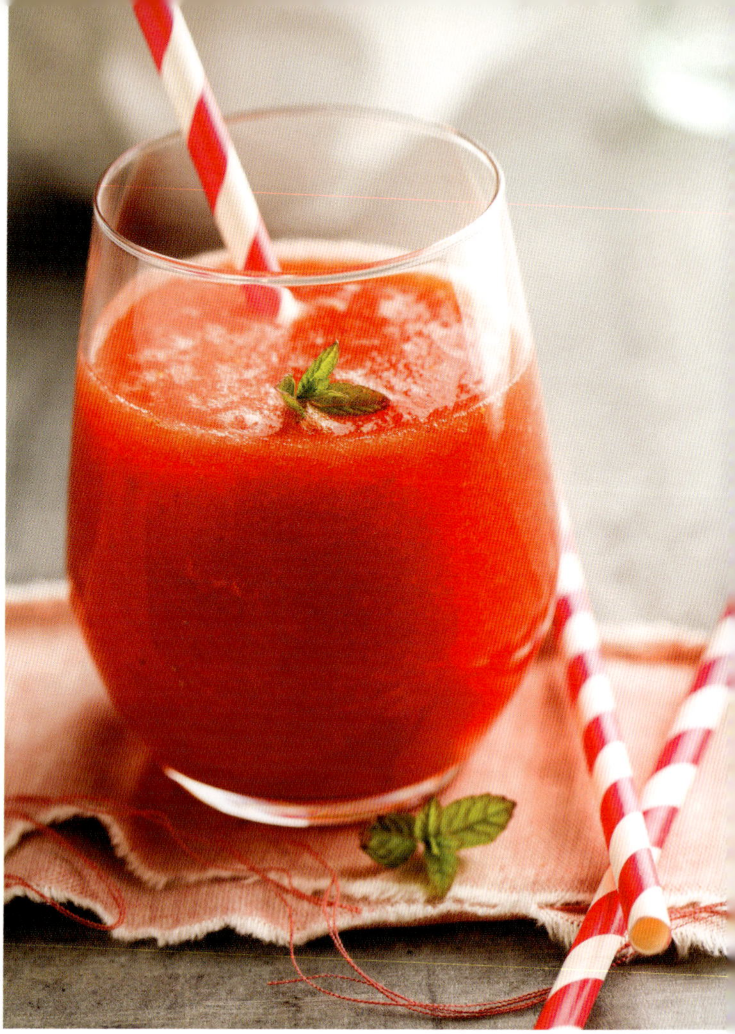

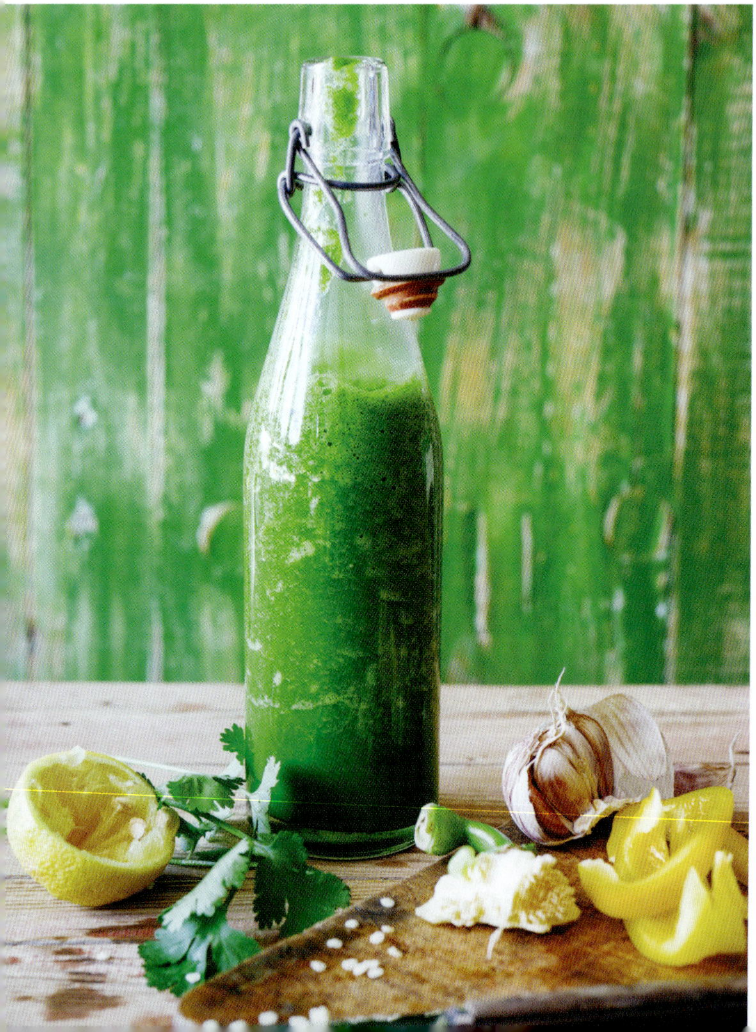

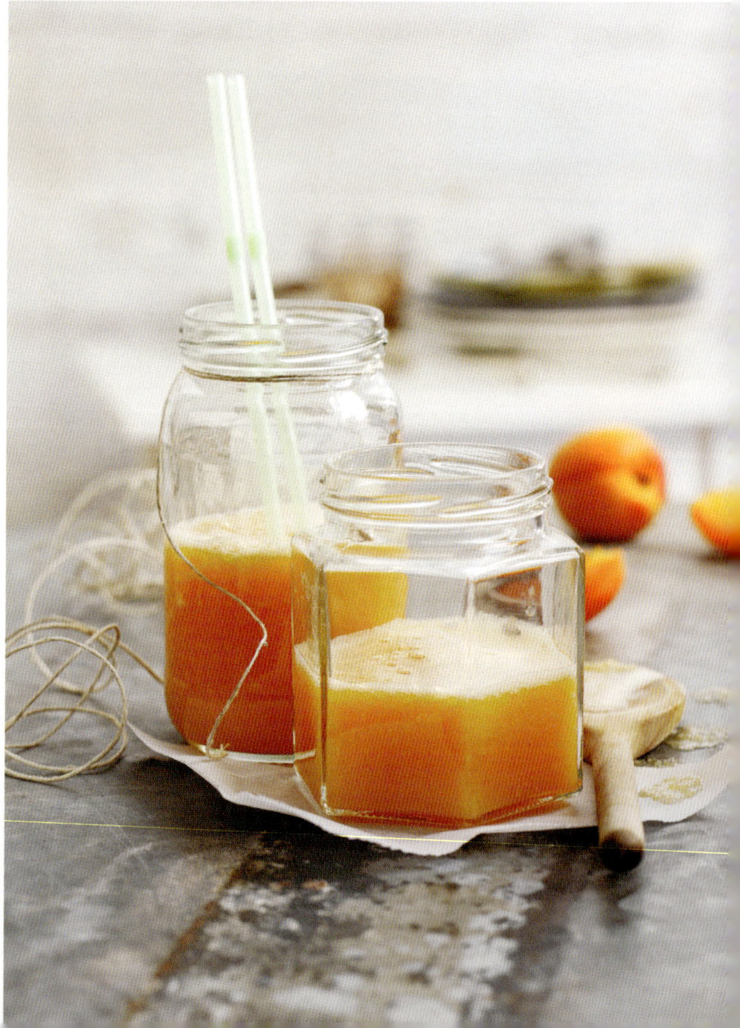

FRUITS AND VEGETABLES

Add colour, flavour and variety to your diet with these healthy, great-tasting fruit and vegetable juices and smoothies. Enjoy sweet fruity combinations, such as Watermelon and Strawberry Refreshing Juice, or more savoury blends such as Black Kale and Wild Garlic Smoothies.

PURPLE CARROT AND STRAWBERRY SMOOTHIES

Serves 4
Preparation 10 minutes

Ingredients:

8 purple carrots, peeled
225 g | 8 oz | 1½ cups strawberries
350 g | 12 oz | 1½ cups natural yoghurt
2 tbsp runny honey
8 ice cubes

Method:

1. Cut eight thin slices from the thick end of one of the carrots, then cut the rest of the carrot lengthways into quarters. Set aside for the garnish. Put the rest of the carrots through a juicer.

2. Cut two strawberries in half and reserve for the garnish, then hull the rest and put them in a blender with the carrot juice, yoghurt, honey and ice cubes.

3. Blend until smooth and divide between four glasses. Top each one with two carrot slices and half a strawberry, then add a quartered carrot as a swizzle stick.

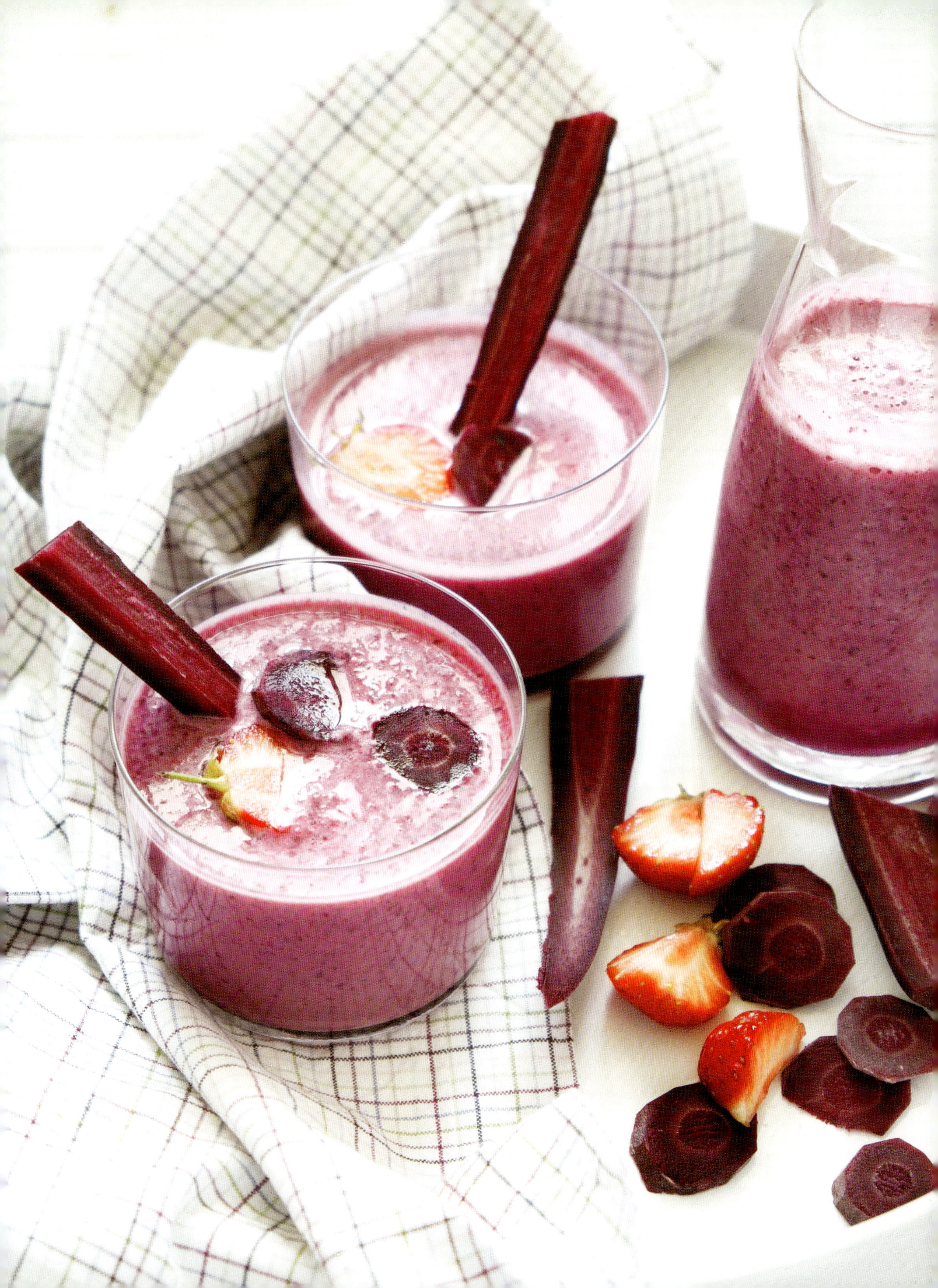

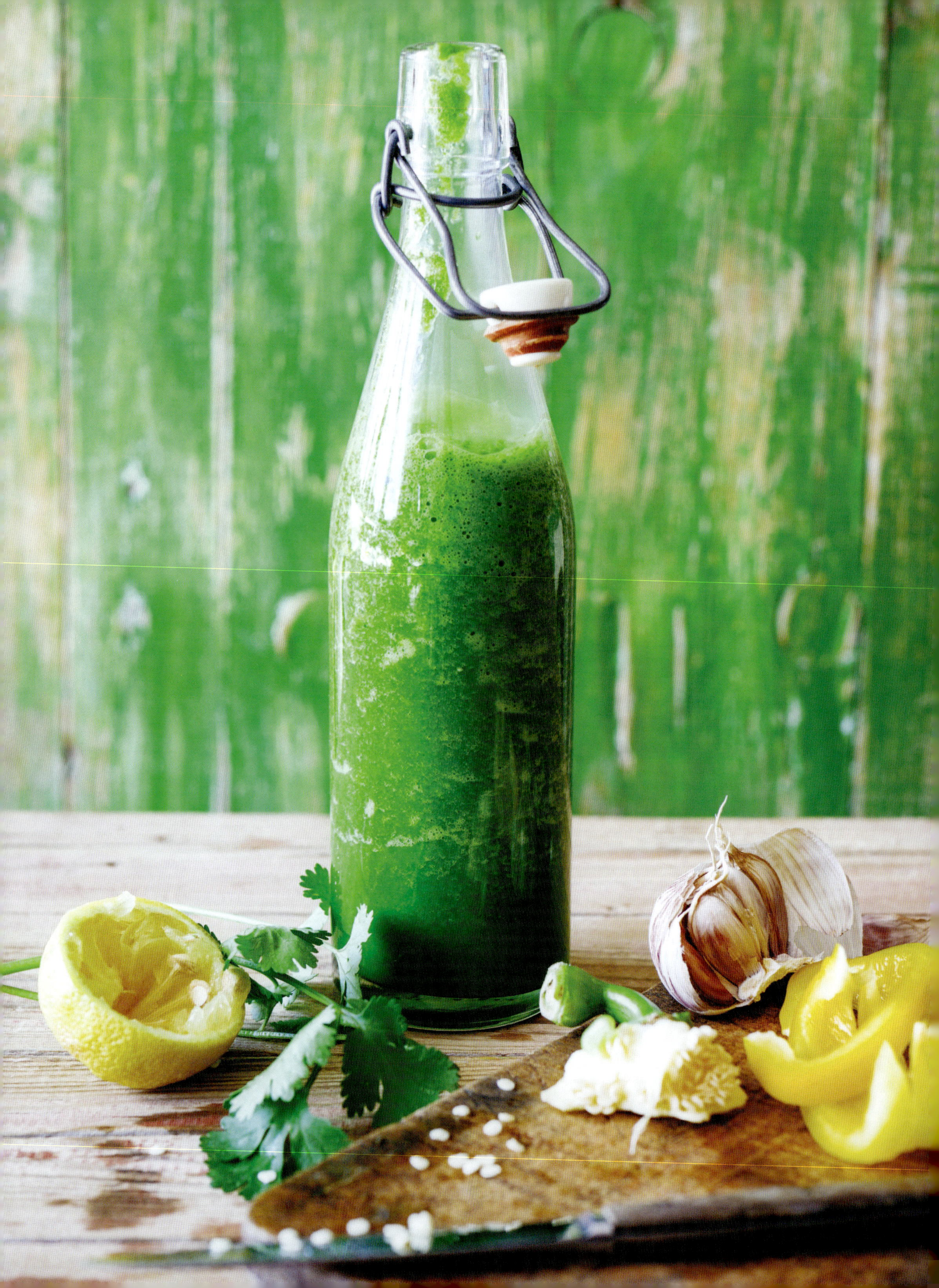

BLACK KALE AND WILD GARLIC SMOOTHIES

Serves 4
Preparation 10 minutes + freezing 2 hours

Ingredients:

3 ripe avocados, peeled, stoned and cubed
2 yellow capsicums (peppers), stalks and seeds removed
1 lemon, juiced
1 clove garlic, crushed
75 g | 2½ oz | 2 cups black kale, stems removed
1 handful fresh coriander (cilantro)
370 ml | 13 fl oz | 1½ cups coconut water

Method:

1. Spread the cubed avocado out on a lined baking tray (sheet) and freeze for 2 hours or until solid.

2. Pass the capsicums (peppers) through a juicer and transfer the juice to a blender with the lemon juice, garlic, kale, coriander (cilantro) and coconut water.

3. Blend until smooth, then add the frozen avocado and blend again.

WATERMELON AND STRAWBERRY REFRESHING JUICE

Serves 2
Preparation 3 minutes

Ingredients:

300 g | 11 oz | 2 cups watermelon, diced
400 g | 14 oz | 2⅔ cups strawberries, hulled
1 cucumber, peeled
2 sprigs mint

Method:

1. Put the watermelon, strawberries and cucumber through a juicer. Stir well, then divide between two glasses and garnish with mint.

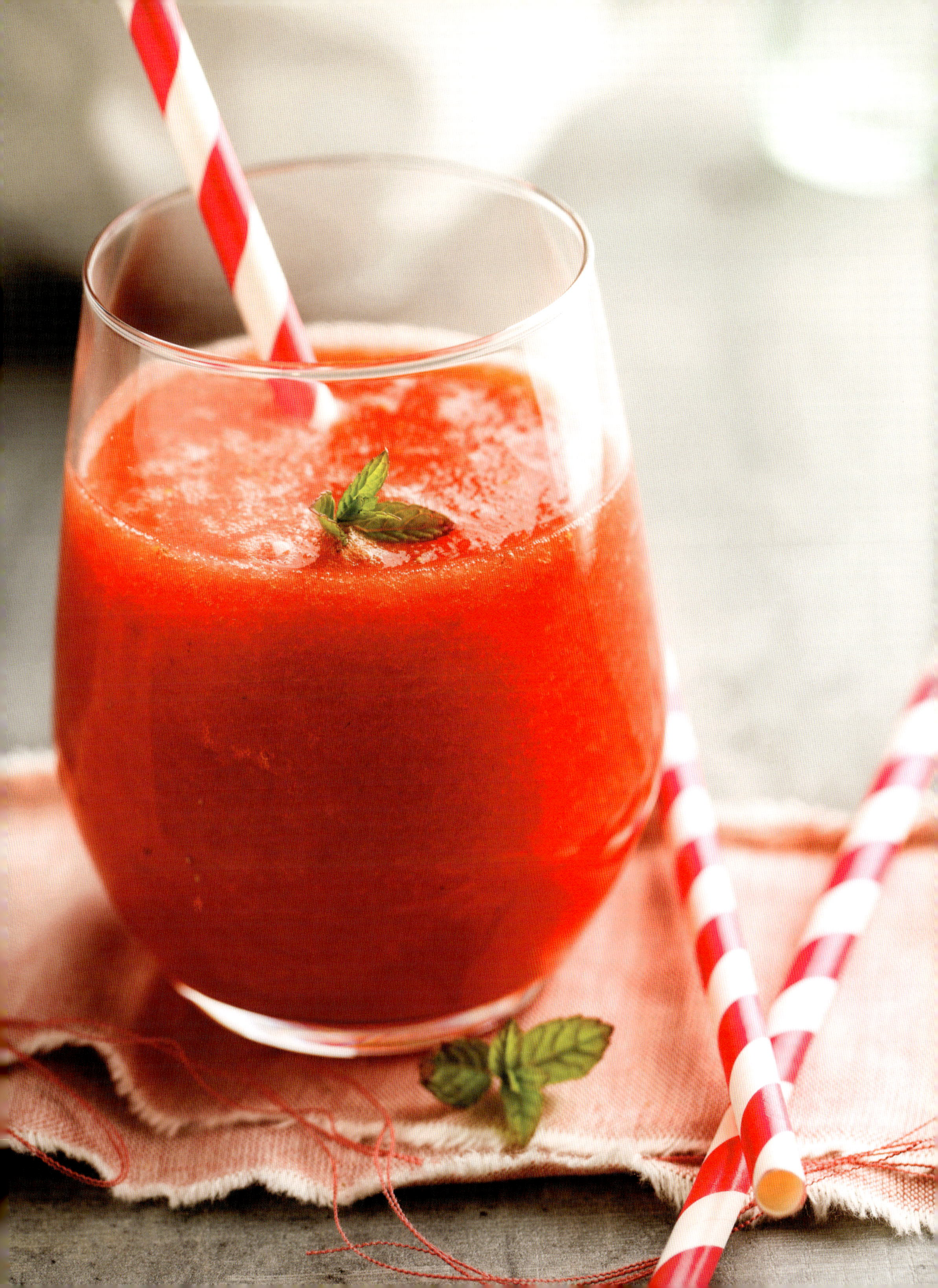

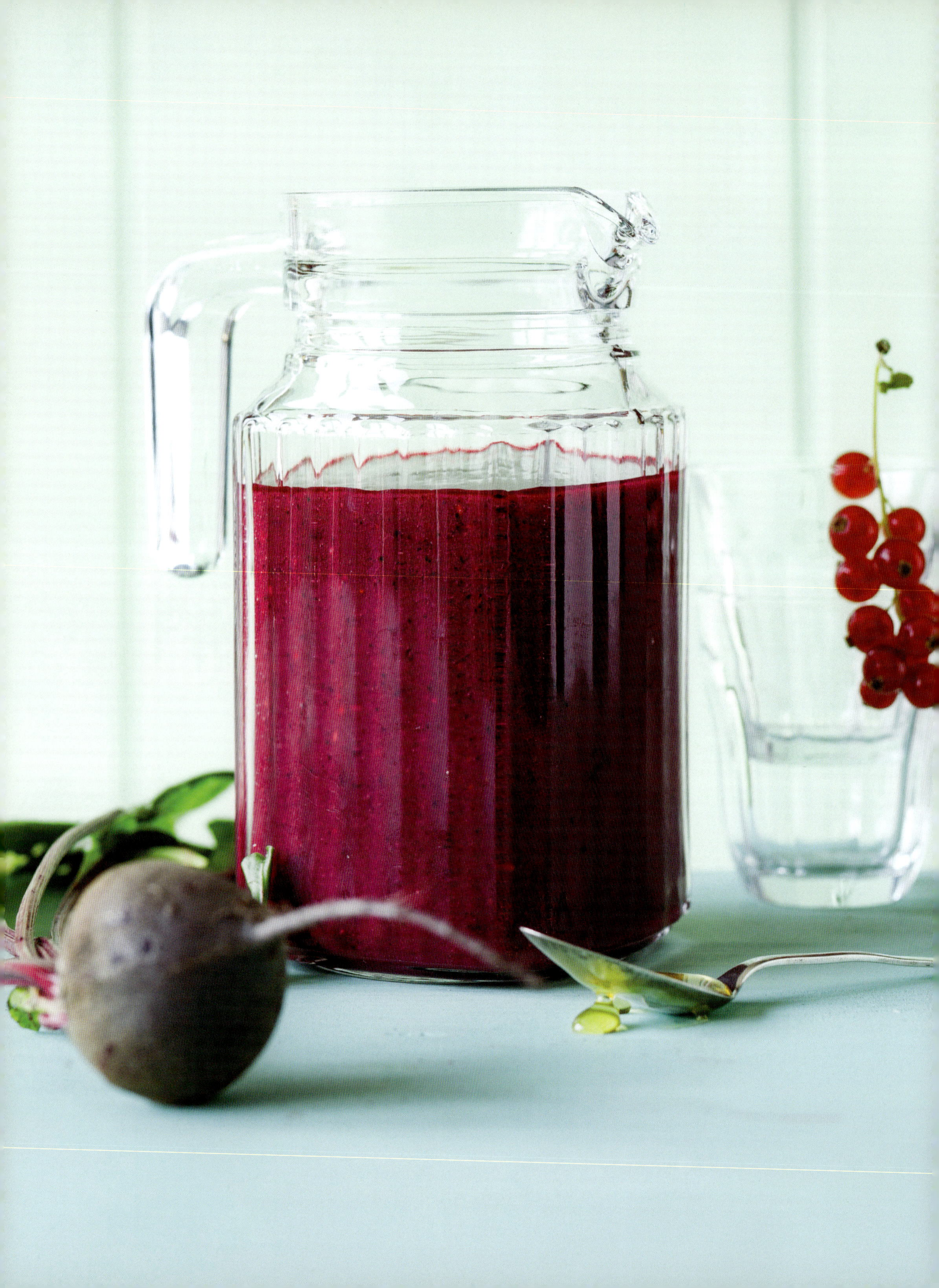

RUBY JUICE

Serves 4
Preparation 3 minutes

Ingredients:

8 medium beetroots (beets), approx. 650 g (23 oz)
4 large oranges, peeled
300 g | 11 oz | 3 cups redcurrants, stems removed
runny honey, to taste

Method:

1. Put the beetroot (beets), oranges and redcurrants through a juicer.

2. Stir well and add honey to taste.

LAYERED JUICE WITH AGAVE AND COCONUT

Serves 3
Preparation 15 minutes + freezing 2 hours

Ingredients:

1 pineapple, peeled and leaves removed
3 mangoes, peeled and stoned
8 beetroots (beets), approx. 650 g (23 oz)
320 ml | 11 fl oz | 1⅓ cups canned coconut cream
2 tbsp light agave nectar
600 ml | 21 fl oz | 2½ cups coconut water, chilled

Method:

1. Juice the pineapple and pour it into an ice cube tray. Juice the mangoes and pour the juice into a second ice cube tray. Juice the beetroots (beets) and pour half of the juice into a third ice cube tray and chill the rest in the fridge. Freeze the juice cubes for 2 hours or until solid.

2. Stir the coconut cream and agave nectar together and chill until ready to serve.

3. Divide the pineapple ice cubes between three tall glasses and top with a third of the coconut cream in small spoonfuls. Top with the mango ice cubes and add another third of the coconut cream. Arrange the beetroot cubes on top, followed by the rest of the coconut cream.

4. Divide the coconut water between the glasses, pouring it gently down the side. Float the beetroot juice on top by pouring it gently over the back of a spoon. Serve immediately.

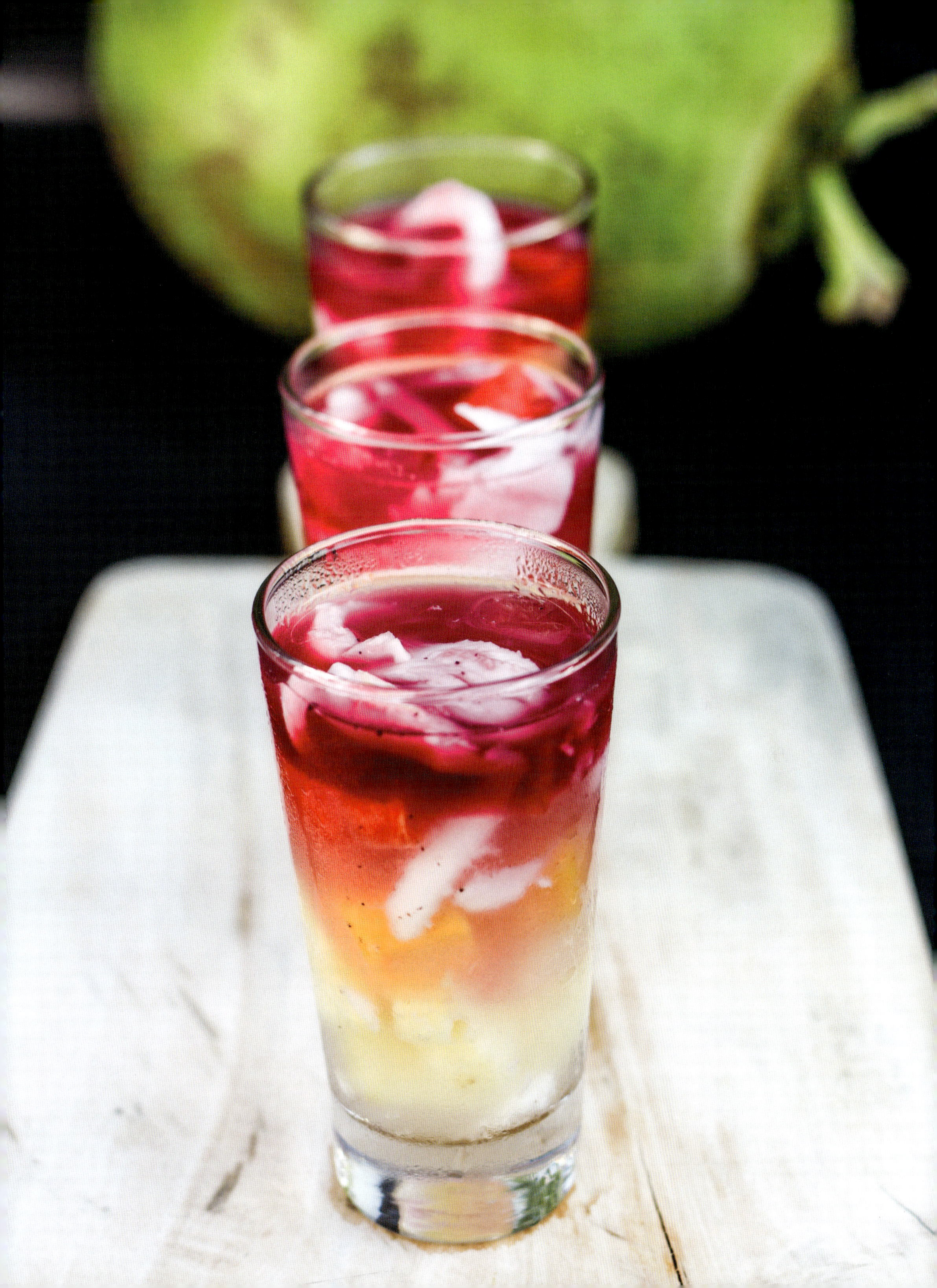

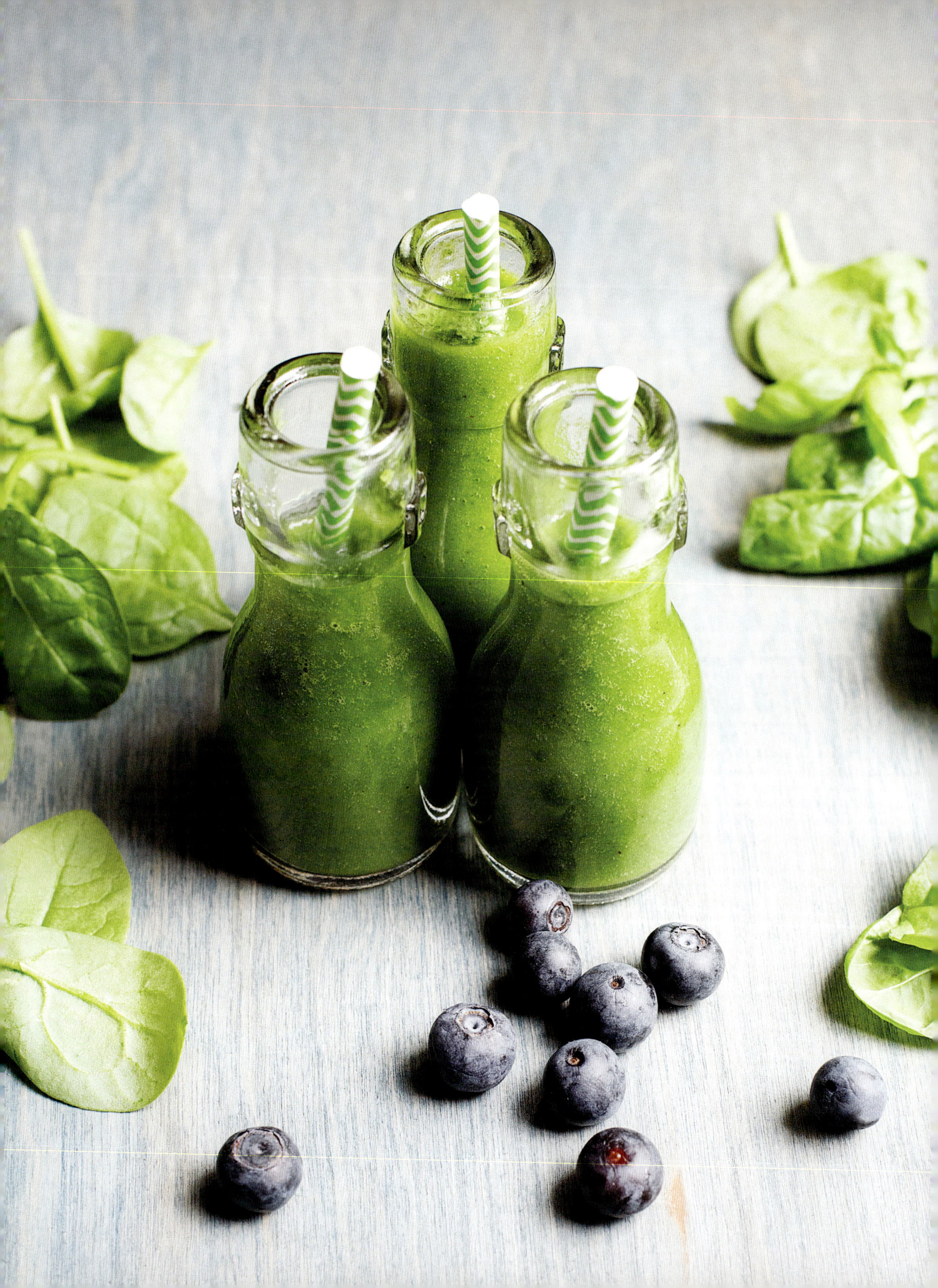

GREEN SMOOTHIES WITH BLUEBERRIES AND WHEATGRASS

Serves 6
Preparation 4 minutes

Ingredients:

35 g | 1¼ oz | 1 cup kale, stems removed
35 g | 1¼ oz | 1 cup baby spinach
1 handful wheatgrass
500 ml | 18 fl oz | 2 cups apple juice
450 g | 16 oz | 3 cups frozen blueberries

Method:

1. Put the kale, spinach and wheatgrass in a blender with the apple juice and blend until smooth.

2. Add the frozen blueberries and blend again until smooth. Serve immediately.

PEAR, APRICOT AND CARROT JUICE

Serves 4
Preparation 15 minutes

Ingredients:

4 firm and juicy pears, peeled, cored and diced
4 ripe apricots, peeled, pitted and diced
4 large carrots, peeled and grated
½ lemon, juiced
500 ml | 18 fl oz | 2 cups cold water

Method:

1. Combine the pears, apricots, carrots, lemon juice and water in a food processor or blender.

2. Blend on high for 2-3 minutes until smooth and frothy.

3. Pour into glasses and serve immediately for best results.

Tip: For a sweeter juice, add a tablespoon of honey before blending.

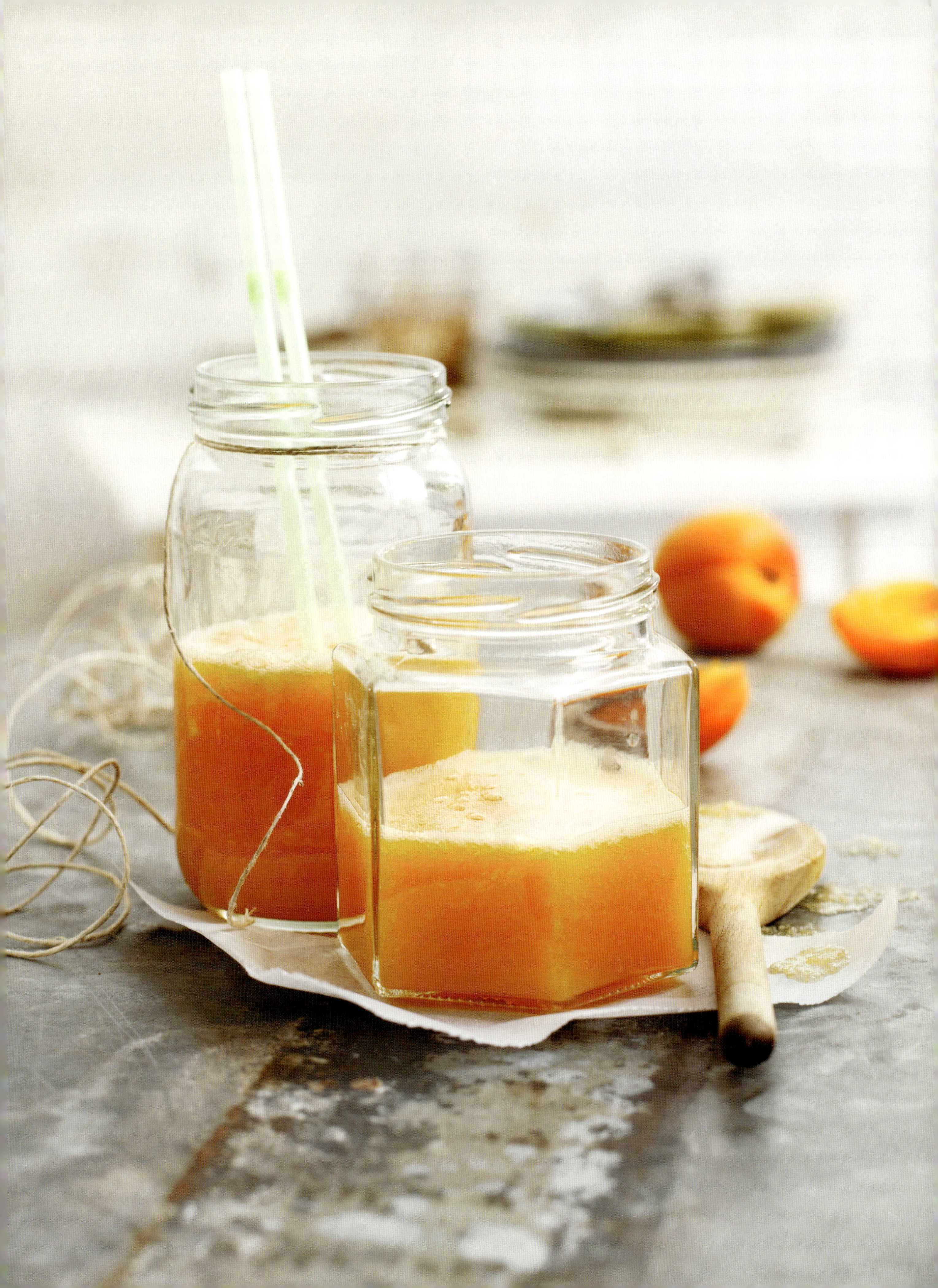

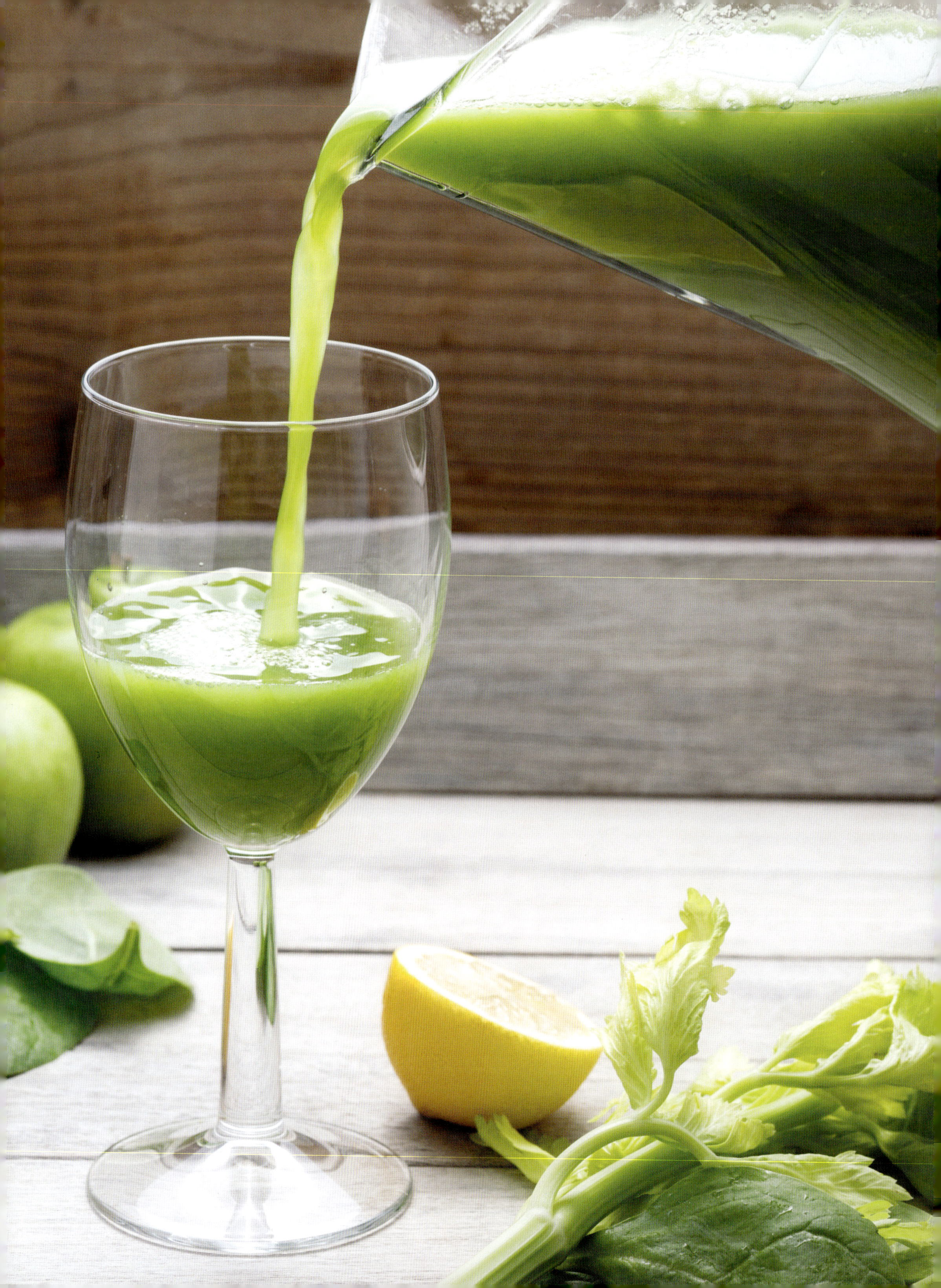

FRESH APPLE AND CELERY JUICE

Serves 4
Preparation 3 minutes

Ingredients:

6 large Granny Smith apples, quartered
8 stalks celery
2 lemons, peeled
30 g | 1 oz | 1 cup baby spinach

Method:

1. Pass the apples, celery, lemons and spinach through a juicer. Stir well and serve immediately.

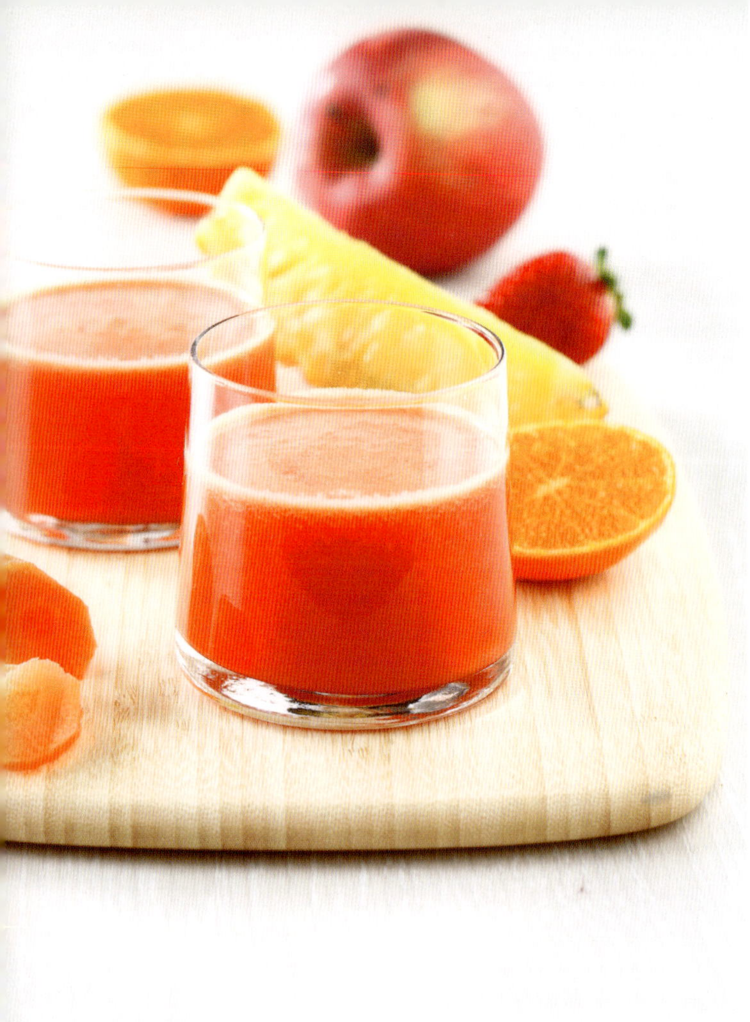
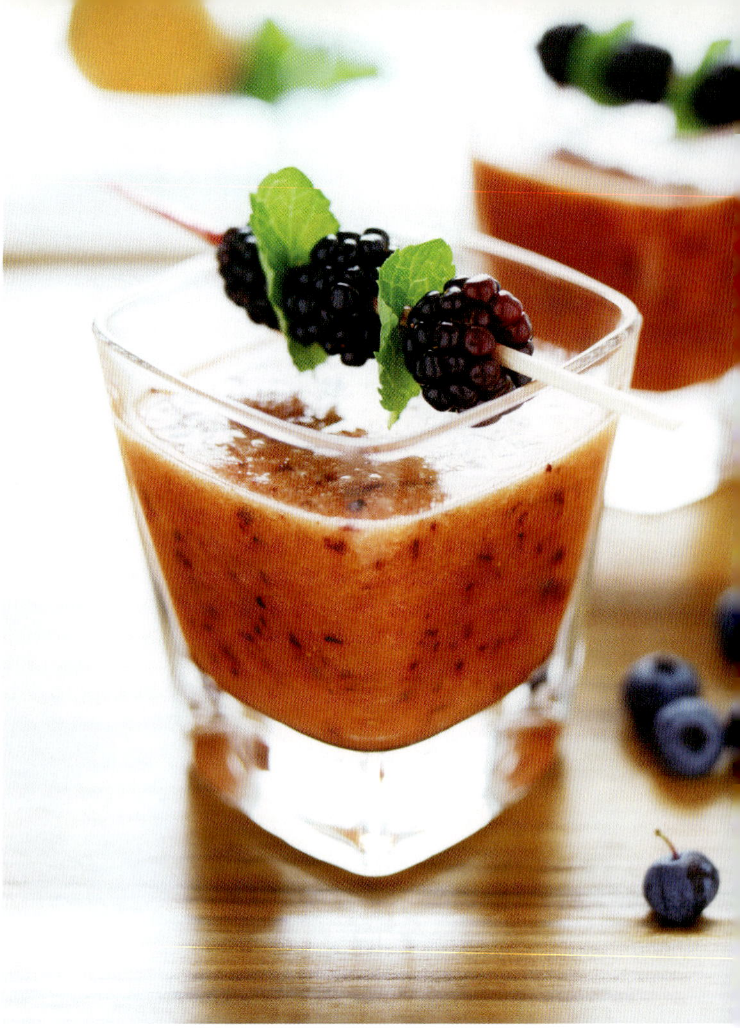
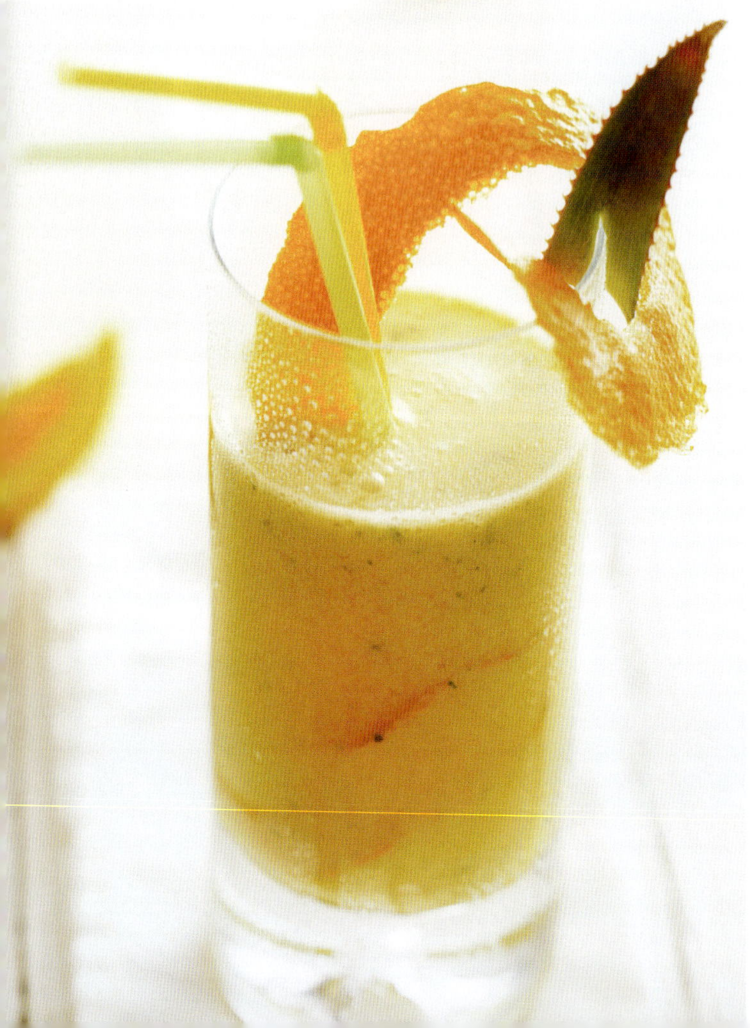
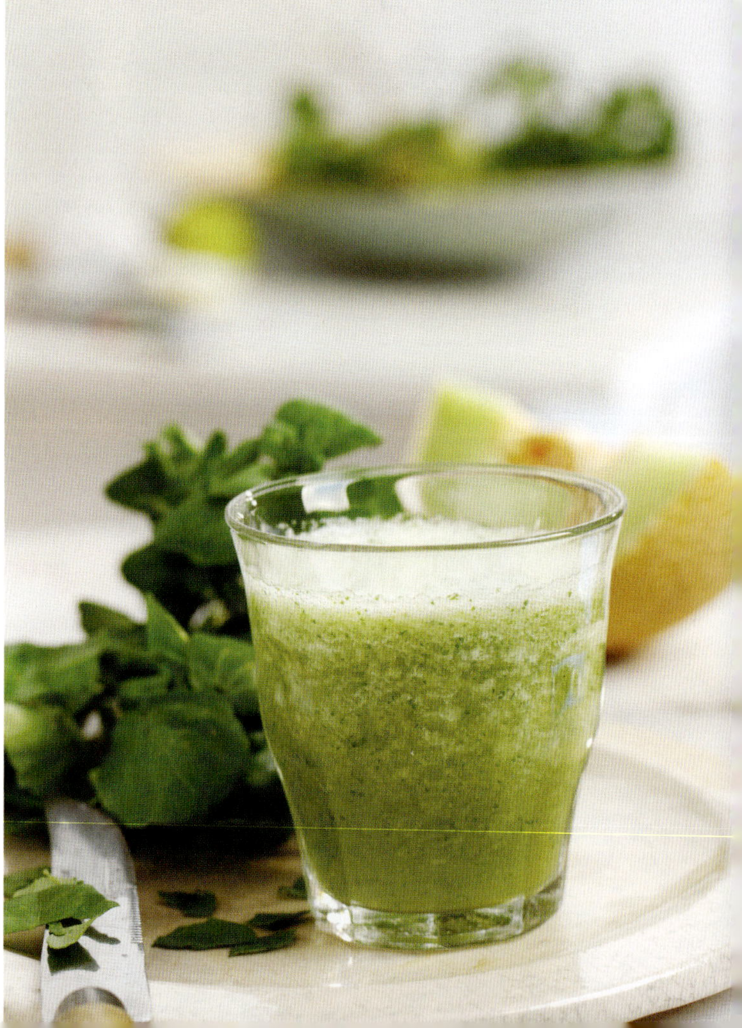

ENERGY BOOSTERS

If you're training for a big sporting event or simply need a pick-me-up, these energy-boosting combinations will soon have you feeling top of your game. Smoothies and juices containing nuts, grains, yoghurt and a wide variety of fresh fruits and vegetables will leave you feeling energised and revitalised.

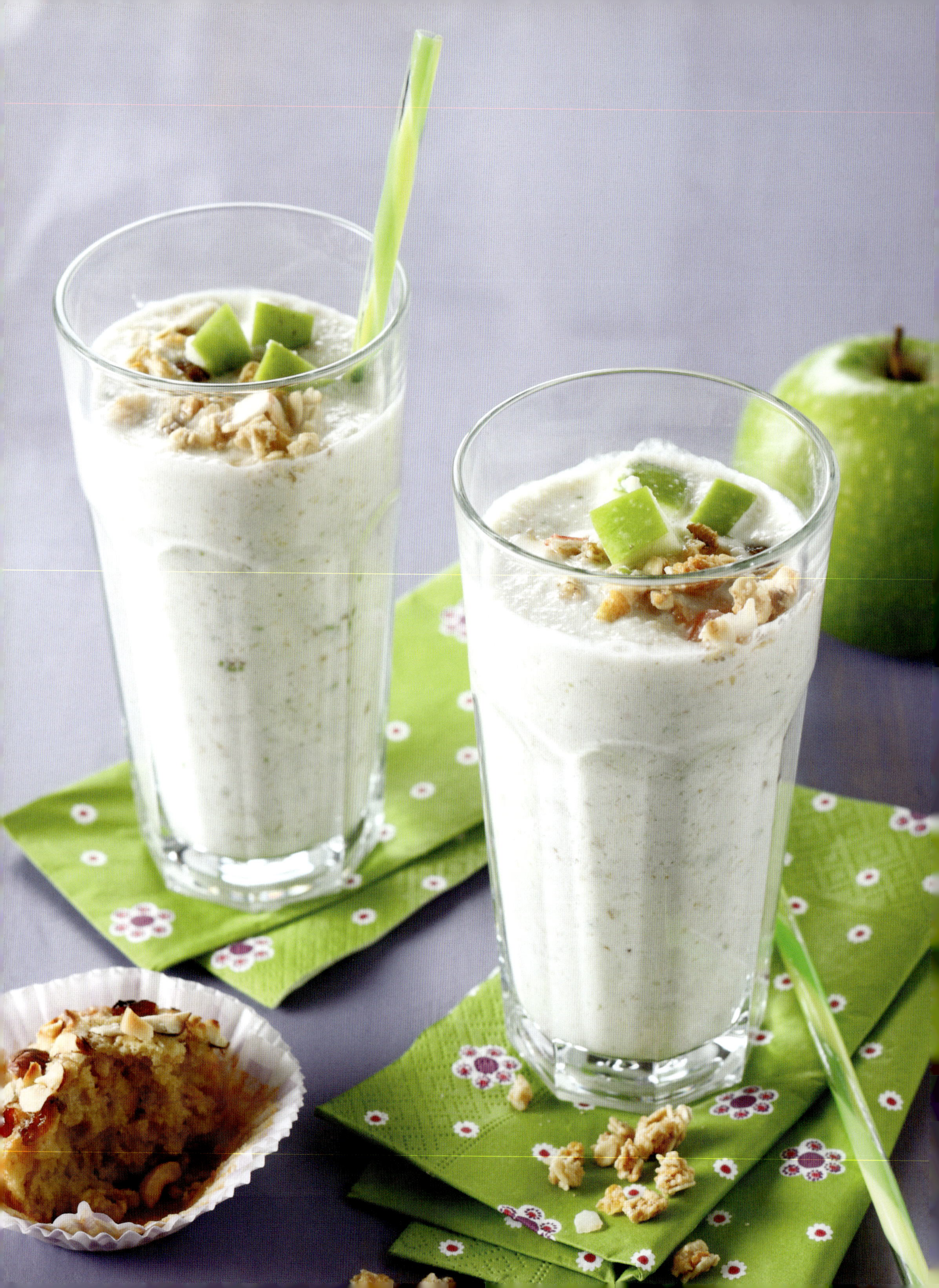

MUESLI AND APPLE SMOOTHIES

Serves 2
Preparation 10 minutes

Ingredients:

1 Granny Smith apple, peeled, cored and diced, 6–8 pieces set aside to garnish
70 g | 2½ oz crunchy spelt muesli
2 tbsp honey
150 g | 5 oz | ⅔ cup natural yoghurt
150 ml | 5 fl oz | ⅔ cup milk

Method:

1. Place the apple, 50 g (1¾ oz) muesli, the honey, yoghurt and milk in a blender and purée well.

2. Pour into two glasses and garnish with the remaining muesli and the set-aside apple.

ENERGISING JUICE

Serves 4
Preparation 4 minutes

Ingredients:

1 pineapple, peeled and leaves removed
4 medium carrots
2 juicy red apples, quartered
4 mandarins, clementines or small oranges, halved
10 medium strawberries

Method:

1. Pass the ingredients through a juicer and stir well before serving.

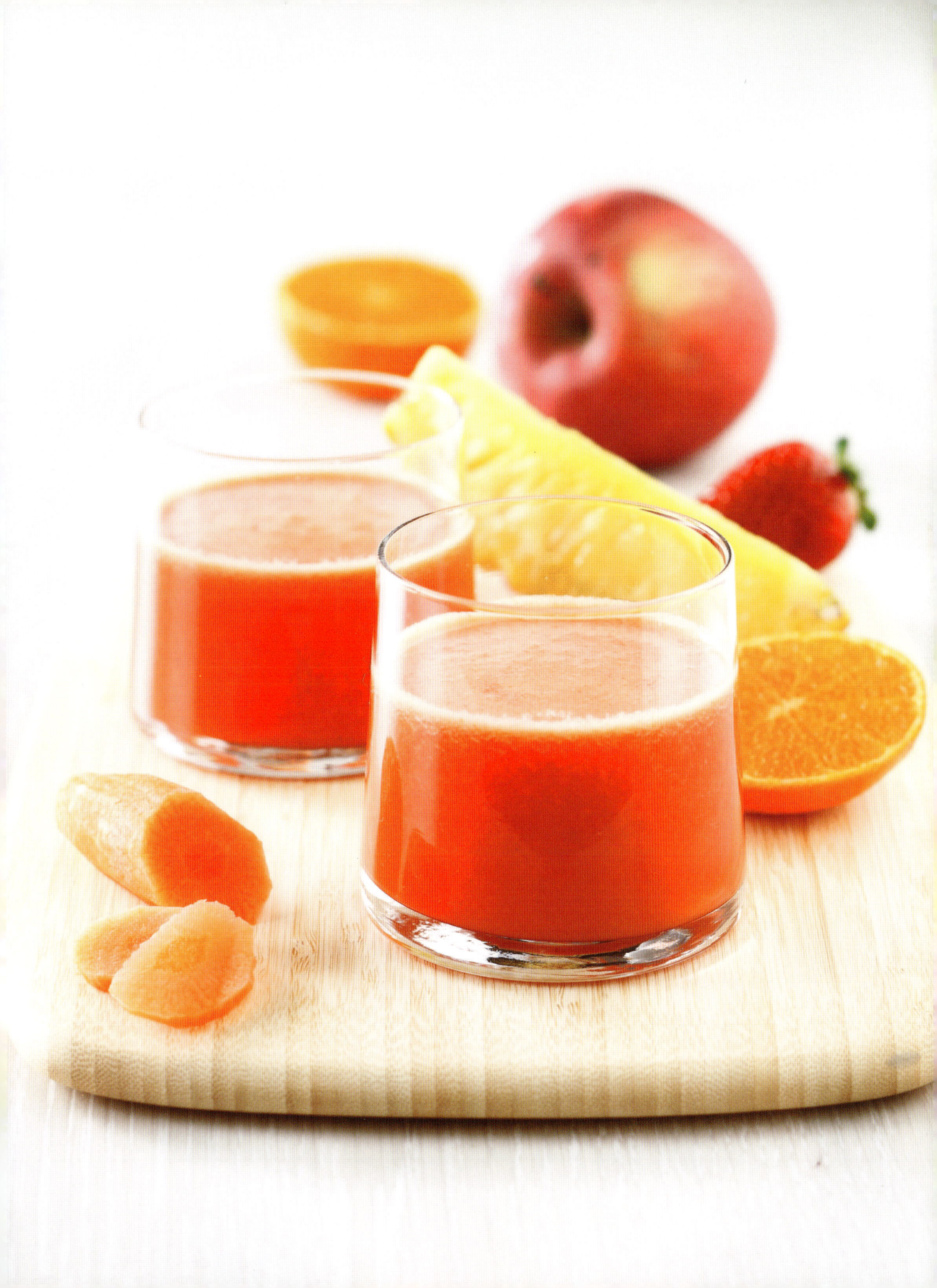

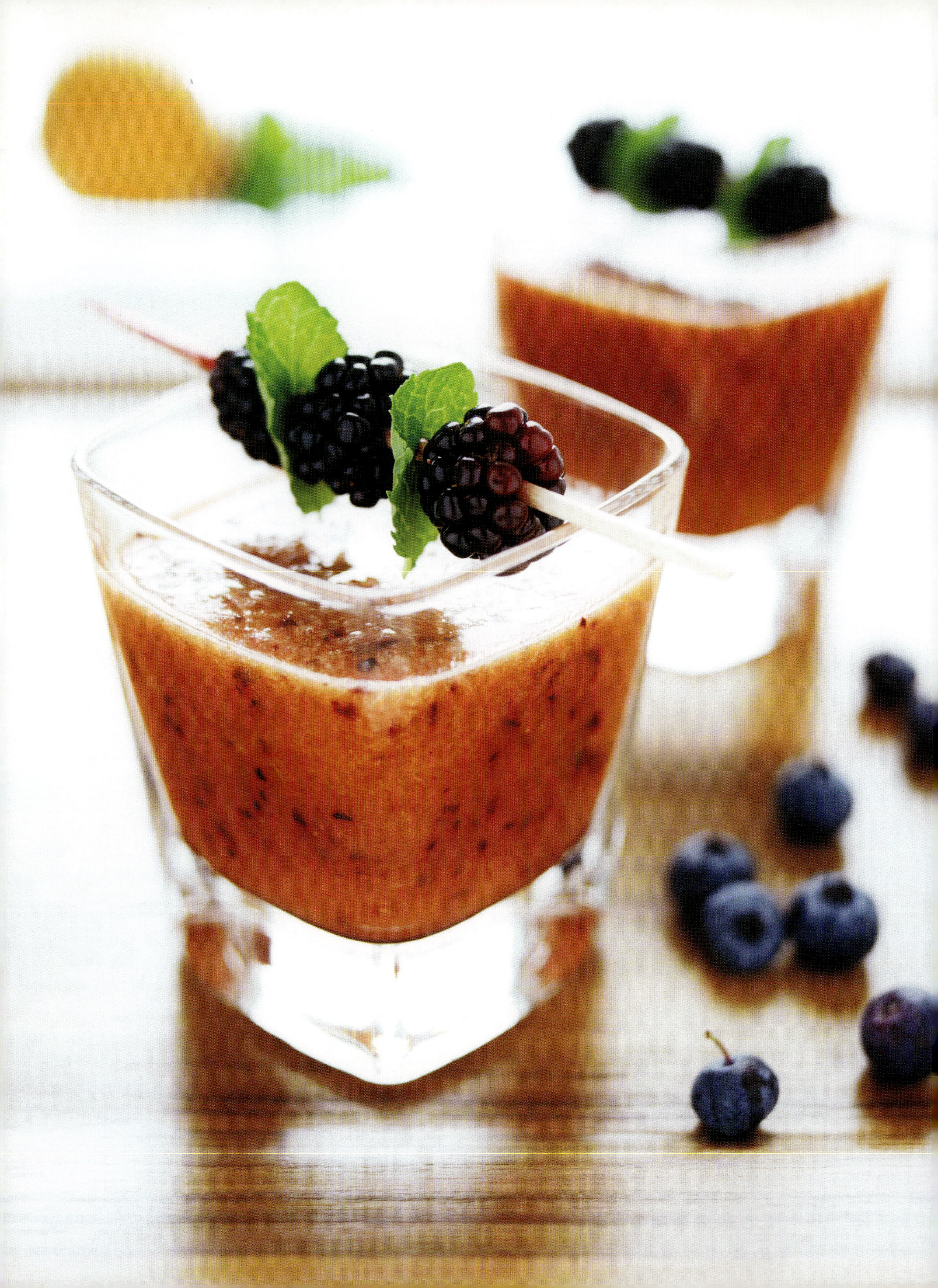

FITNESS SMOOTHIES WITH OAT BRAN

Serves 2
Preparation 10 minutes

Ingredients:

100 g | 3½ oz | ½ cup mixed berries, (e.g. strawberries, blackberries, blueberries) sorted, washed and carefully dried
2 oranges, juiced
2 tbsp lemon juice
100 ml | 3⅓ fl oz carrot juice
1 tsp wheatgerm or rice bran oil
1 tbsp oat bran
1 tbsp honey

Garnish:
6 blackberries threaded onto 2 wooden skewers

Method:

1. Place the berries, orange juice, lemon juice and carrot juice in a blender and blend thoroughly.

2. Add the oil, oat bran and honey and blend well again.

3. Pour the drink into two small glasses and serve garnished with the blackberry skewers.

ORANGE AND ALOE JUICE

Serves 4
Preparation 3 minutes

Ingredients:

6 large oranges
4 stems aloe vera
½ pineapple, peeled and leaves removed

Method:

1. Peel the oranges with a vegetable peeler and choose four long curls for the garnish. Discard the rest of the skin.

2. Cut the tips off the aloe stems and reserve as a garnish. Cut the rest in half lengthways and use a teaspoon to scrape out the clear gel from inside, being careful to leave the yellow latex near the skin behind.

3. Put the aloe gel and orange flesh through a juicer, followed by the pineapple. Stir well and divide between four glasses before garnishing with the reserved orange peel and aloe tips.

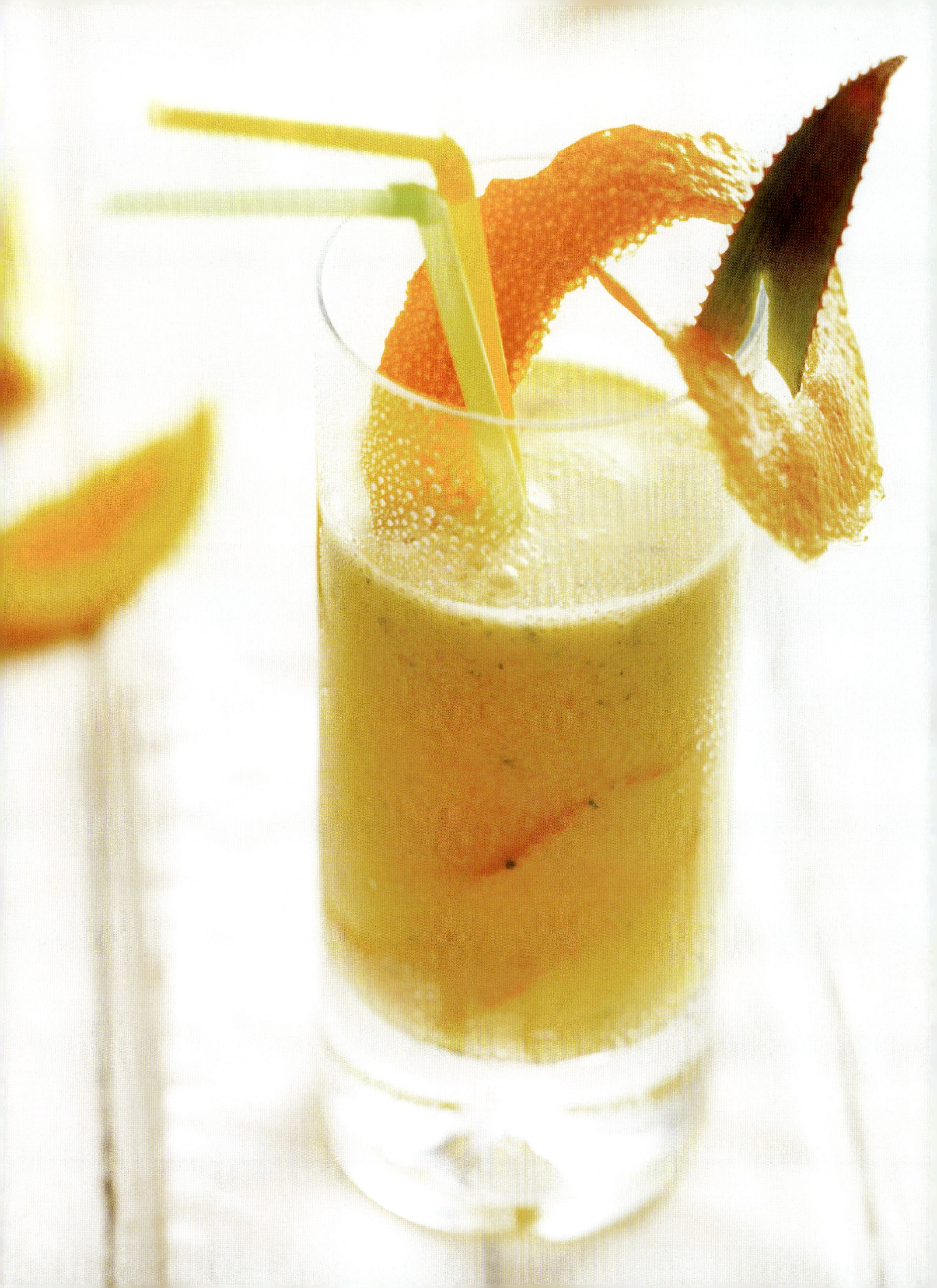

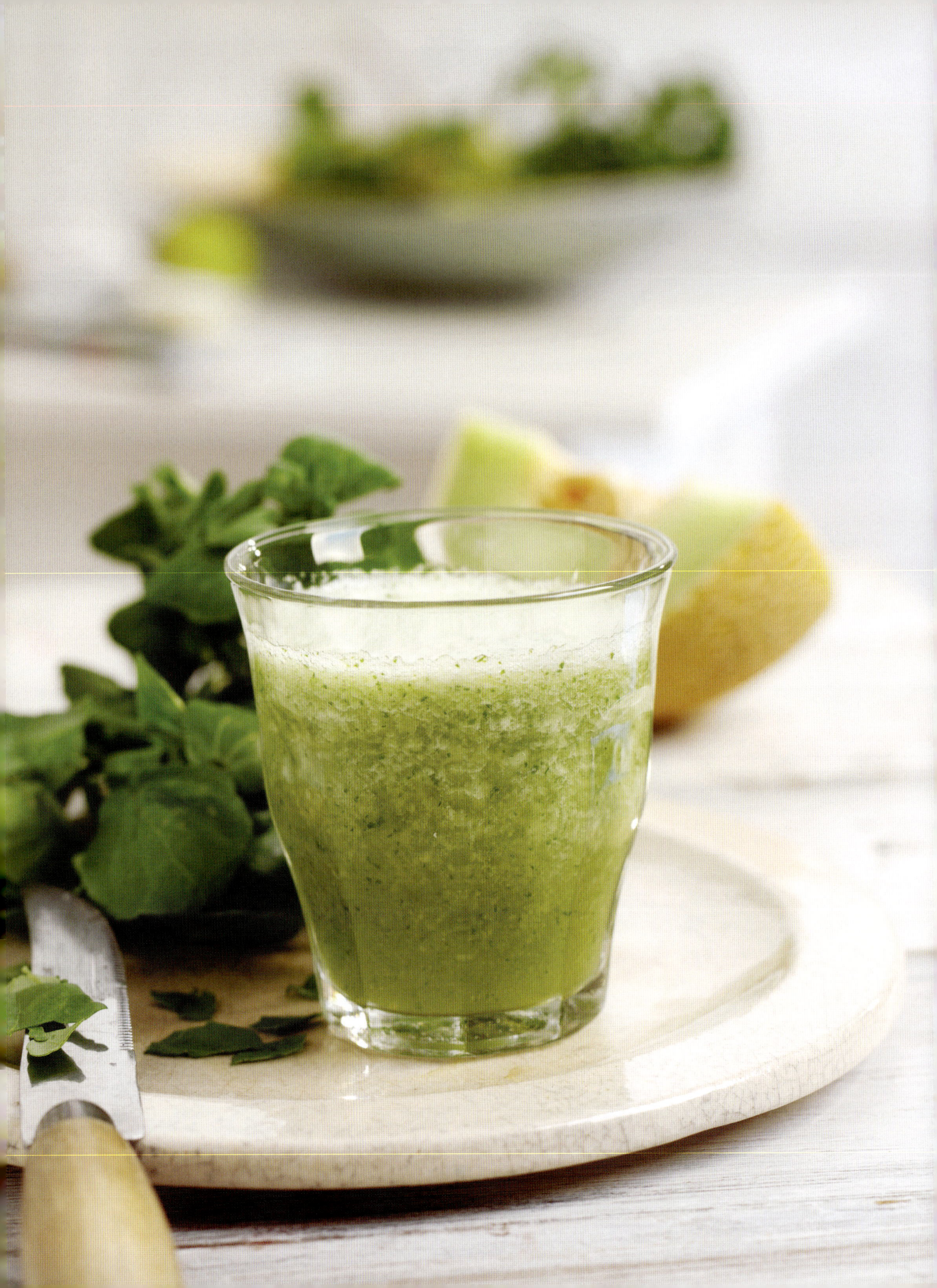

WATERCRESS COCKTAIL WITH MELON AND PEARS

Serves 4
Preparation 4 minutes

Ingredients:

1 honeydew melon, cut into chunks
4 pears, quartered
30 g | 1 oz | 1 cup watercress
1 lemon, quartered

Method:

1. Pass the ingredients through a juicer and stir well before serving.

STRAWBERRY AND ALMOND SMOOTHIES

Serves 2
Preparation 10 minutes + freezing 30 minutes

Ingredients:

200 g | 7 oz | 1 cup ripe strawberries
2 tbsp ground almonds
1 tbsp almond syrup
1 tbsp strawberry syrup, for colour (or more if required)
300 g | 11 oz | 1⅓ cups cold plain yoghurt

Garnish:
Flaked almonds
Strawberry slices

Method:

1. Lay the strawberries in a shallow dish and place in the freezer for 30 minutes to freeze slightly.

2. Purée the strawberries with the ground almonds, both syrups and the yoghurt to a creamy consistency.

3. Divide between two glasses.

4. Garnish with flaked almonds and strawberry slices.

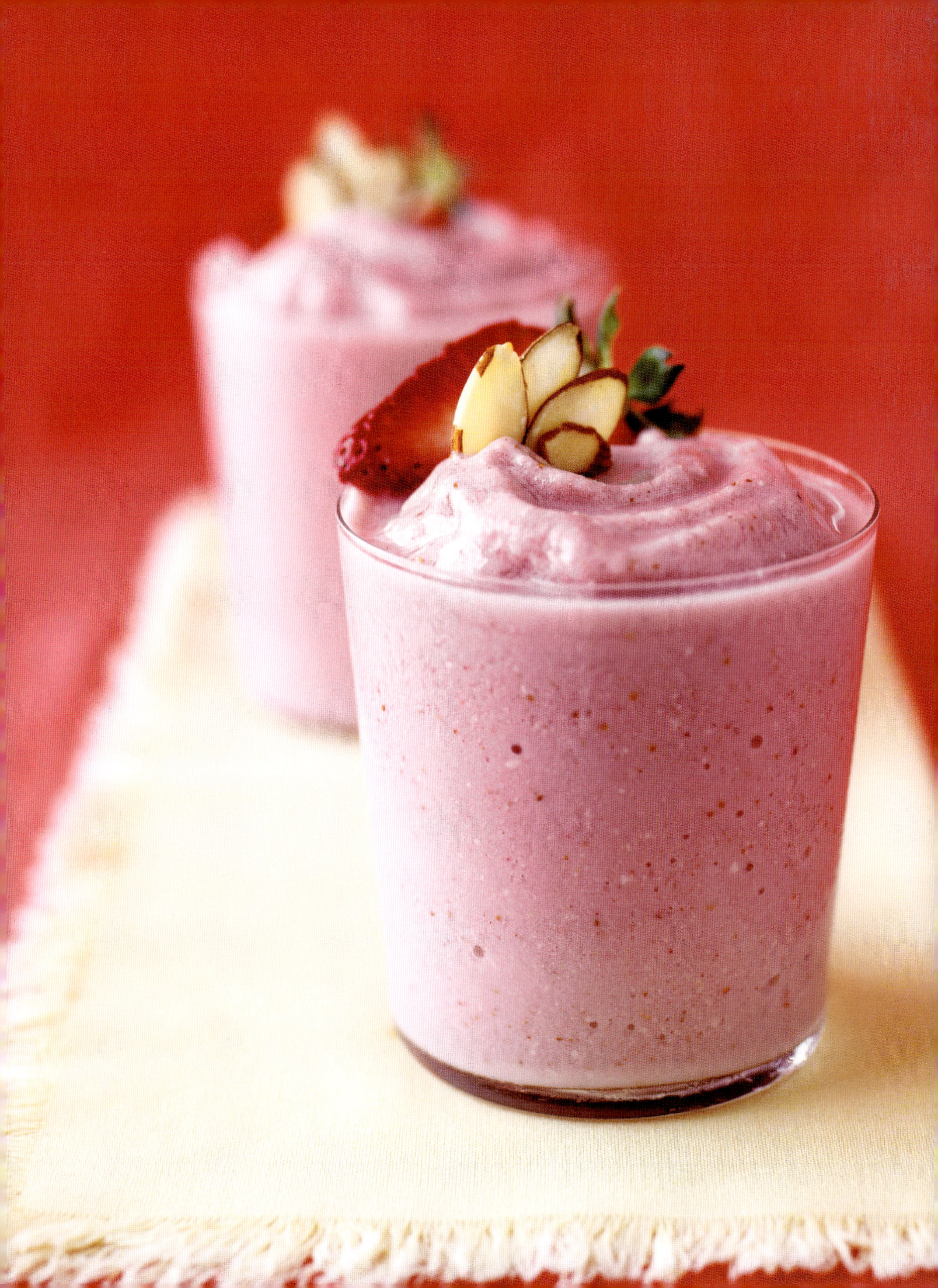

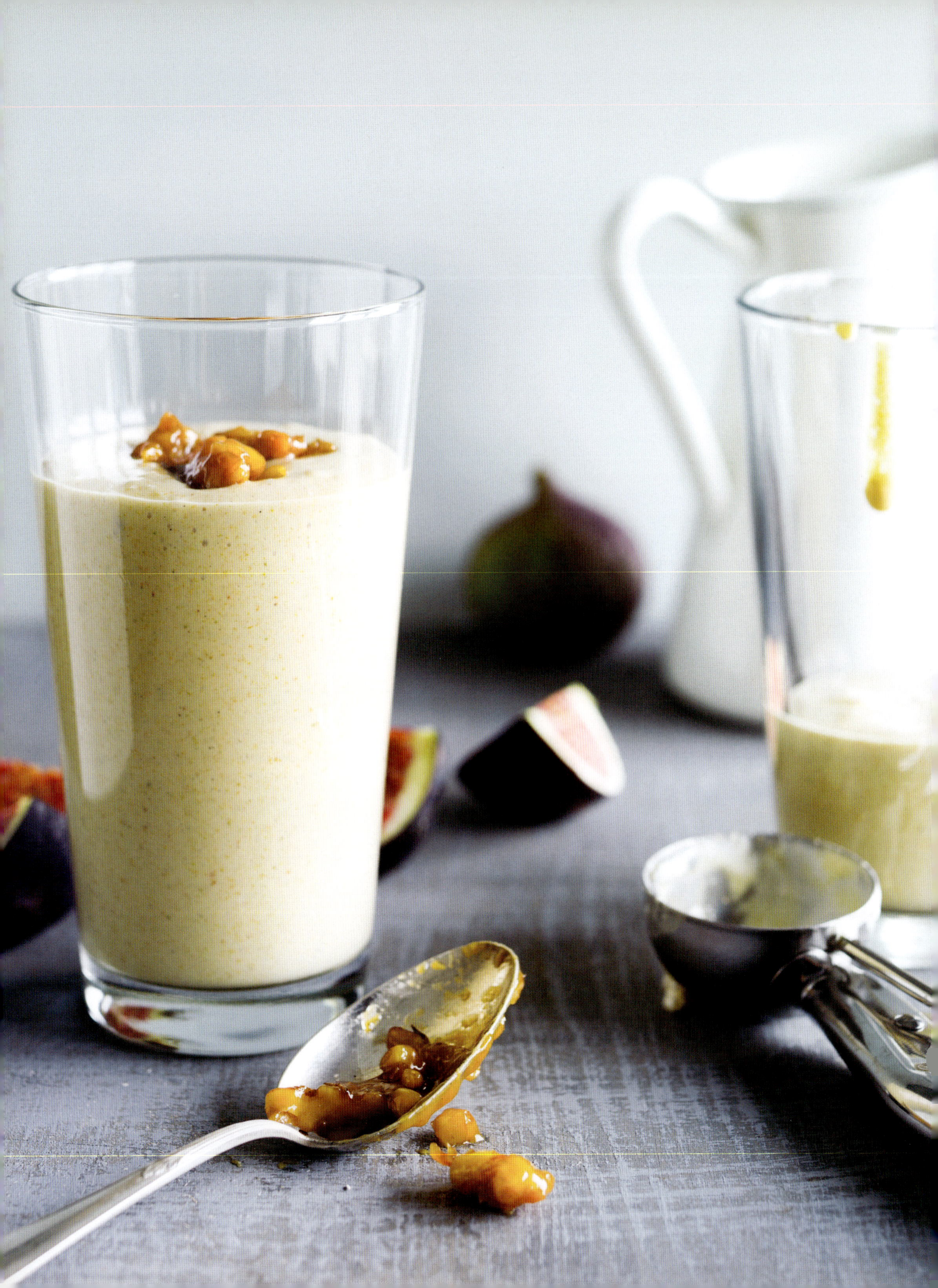

FIG AND WALNUT SMOOTHIES

Serves 4
Preparation and cooking 10 minutes + cooling 20 minutes

Ingredients:

150 g | 5 oz | ½ cup runny honey
100 g | 3½ oz | ⅔ cup walnuts, chopped
8 fresh figs, quartered
1 tsp ground cinnamon
250 ml | 9 fl oz | 1 cup almond milk
500 ml | 18 fl oz | 2 cups fat-free frozen yoghurt

Method:

1. Put the honey and walnuts in a small saucepan and heat together gently for 3 minutes to soften the walnuts. Leave to cool to room temperature.

2. Set aside a tablespoon of the walnut and honey mixture and scrape the rest into a blender with the figs and cinnamon. Blend to a smooth paste.

3. Add the almond milk and frozen yoghurt and blend again until smooth. Divide between four glasses, then spoon the rest of the honeyed walnuts on top.

MANDARIN AND PASSIONFRUIT SMOOTHIES

Serves 2
Preparation 8 minutes + freezing 2 hours

Ingredients:

4 mandarins, peeled and segmented
8 passionfruit, pulp sieved to remove the seeds
50 g | 1¾ oz | ½ cup walnut halves
180 ml | 6 fl oz | ¾ cup almond milk
30 g | 1 oz | 1 cup oakleaf or butter lettuce
15 g | ½ oz | ½ cup rocket (arugula)

Method:

1. Spread out the mandarin segments on a lined baking sheet and freeze for 2 hours or until solid.

2. Put the passionfruit pulp and walnut halves in a blender and blend to a smooth paste, pausing to scrape down the sides if necessary.

3. Add the almond milk, lettuce and rocket and blend until smooth, then add the frozen mandarin segments and blend again. Serve immediately.

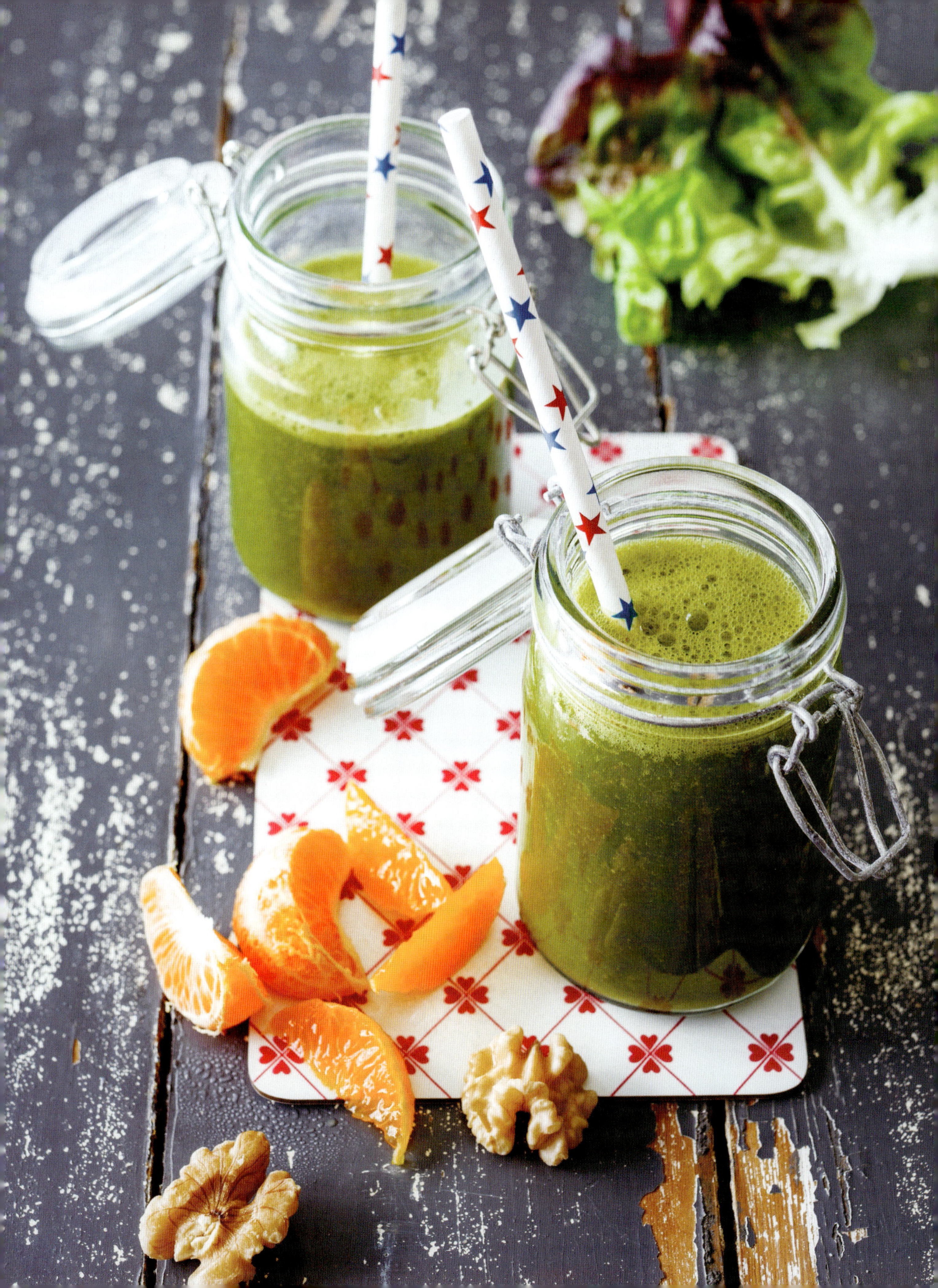

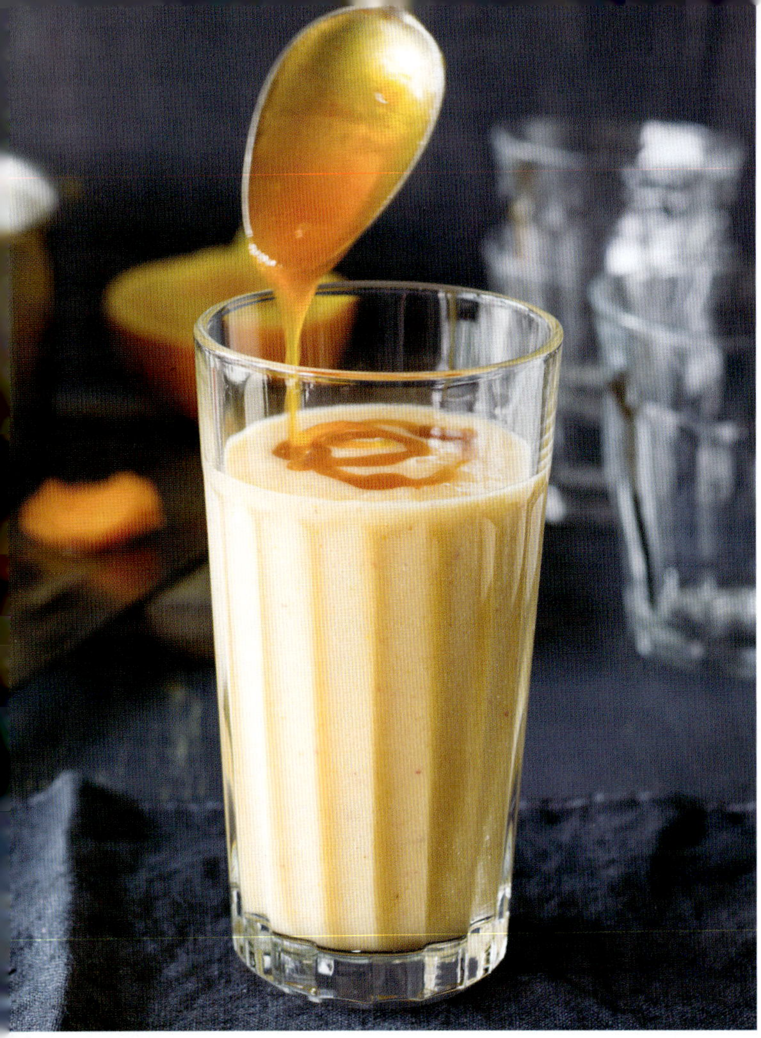
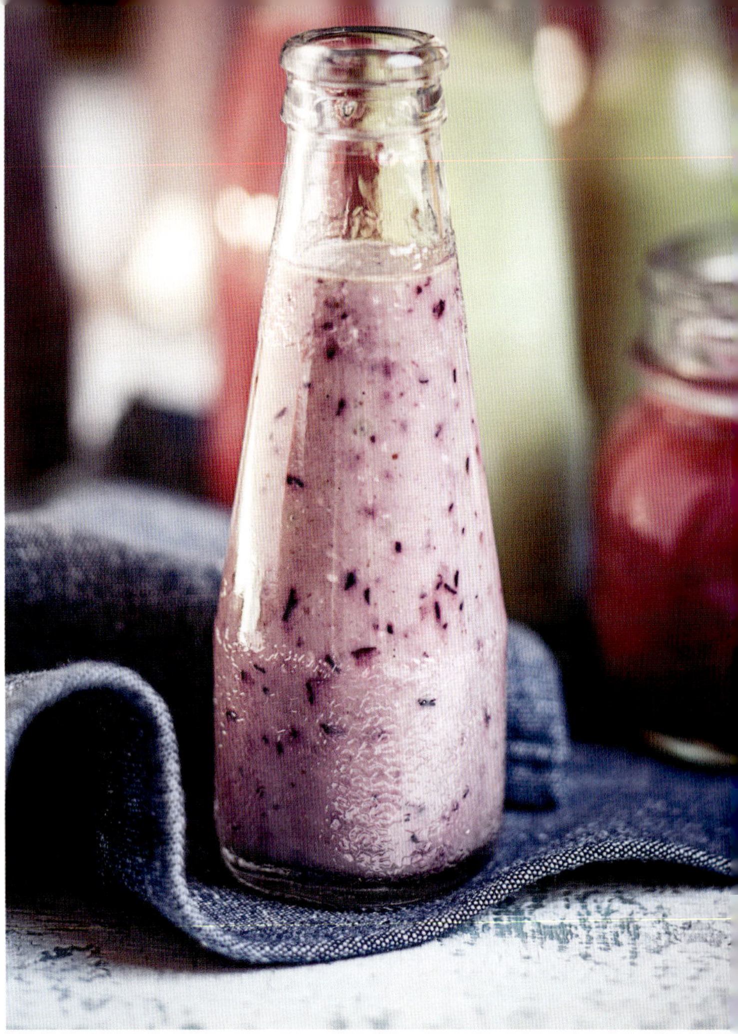
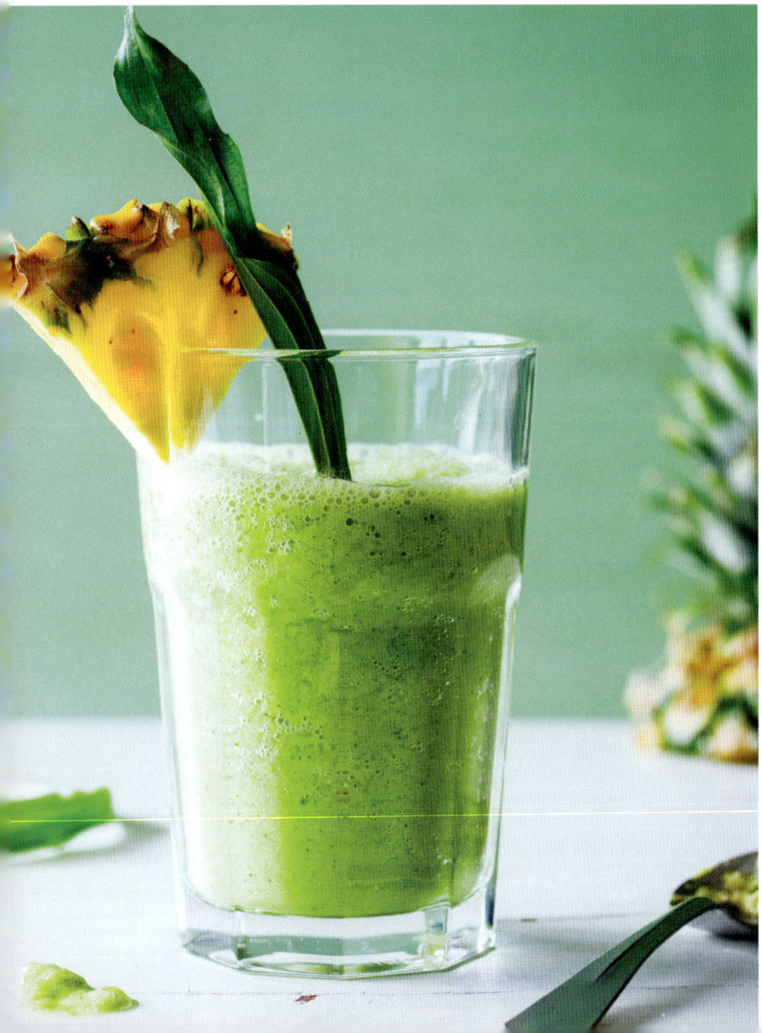
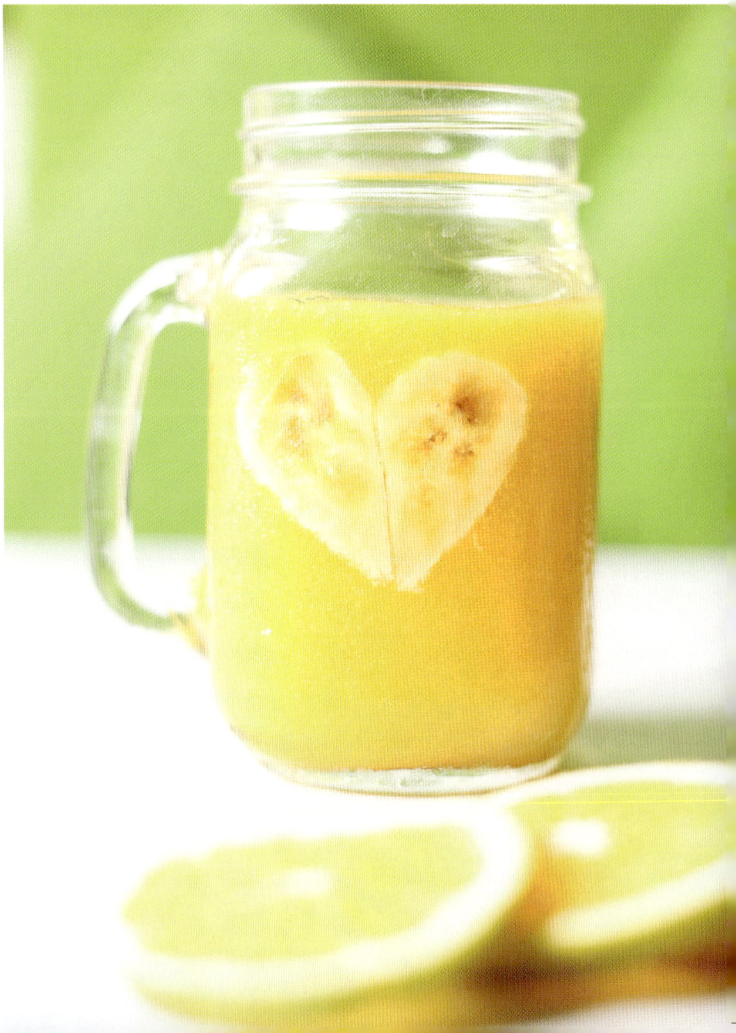

HEALING ELIXIRS

Whether your immune system needs a boost, you're feeling stressed, you're suffering from sore joints or you've overindulged in alcohol, you can find a healing elixir to help get you back on track. These restorative juice and smoothie recipes include nutrient-rich Vegetable Juice, delicious Spicy Buttermilk and Mango Smoothies and soothing Hot Apple Juice with Cinnamon and Ginger. Of course, always consult your doctor before making any significant dietary changes.

VEGETABLE JUICE

Immune booster

Serves 4
Preparation 4 minutes

Ingredients:

6 large carrots
4 red capsicums (peppers)
4 stalks celery
1 leek
1 handful flatleaf parsley
½ tsp Worcester sauce

Method:

1. Pass the carrots, capsicum (pepper), celery, leek and parsley through a juicer. Stir in the Worcester sauce and serve immediately.

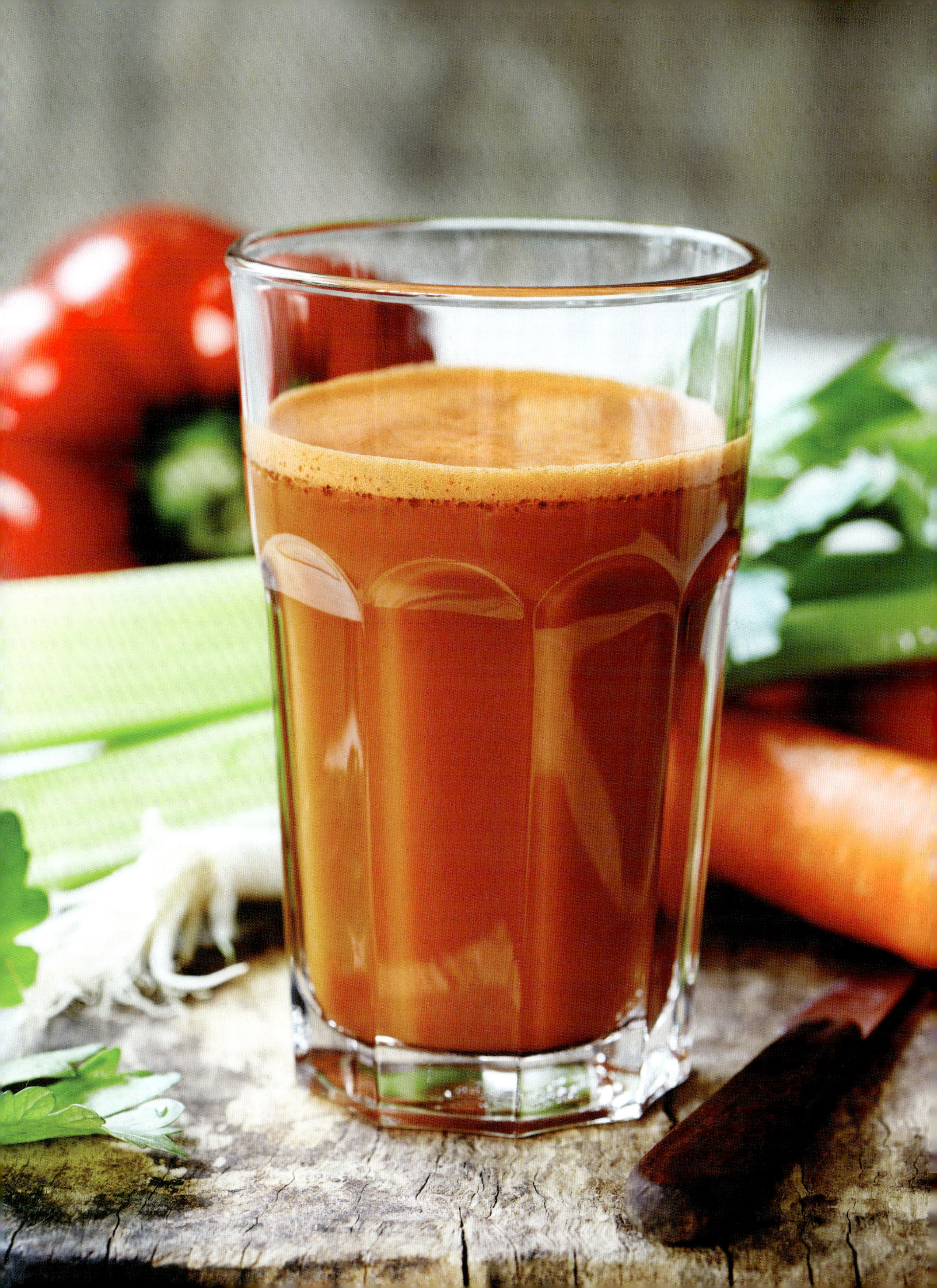

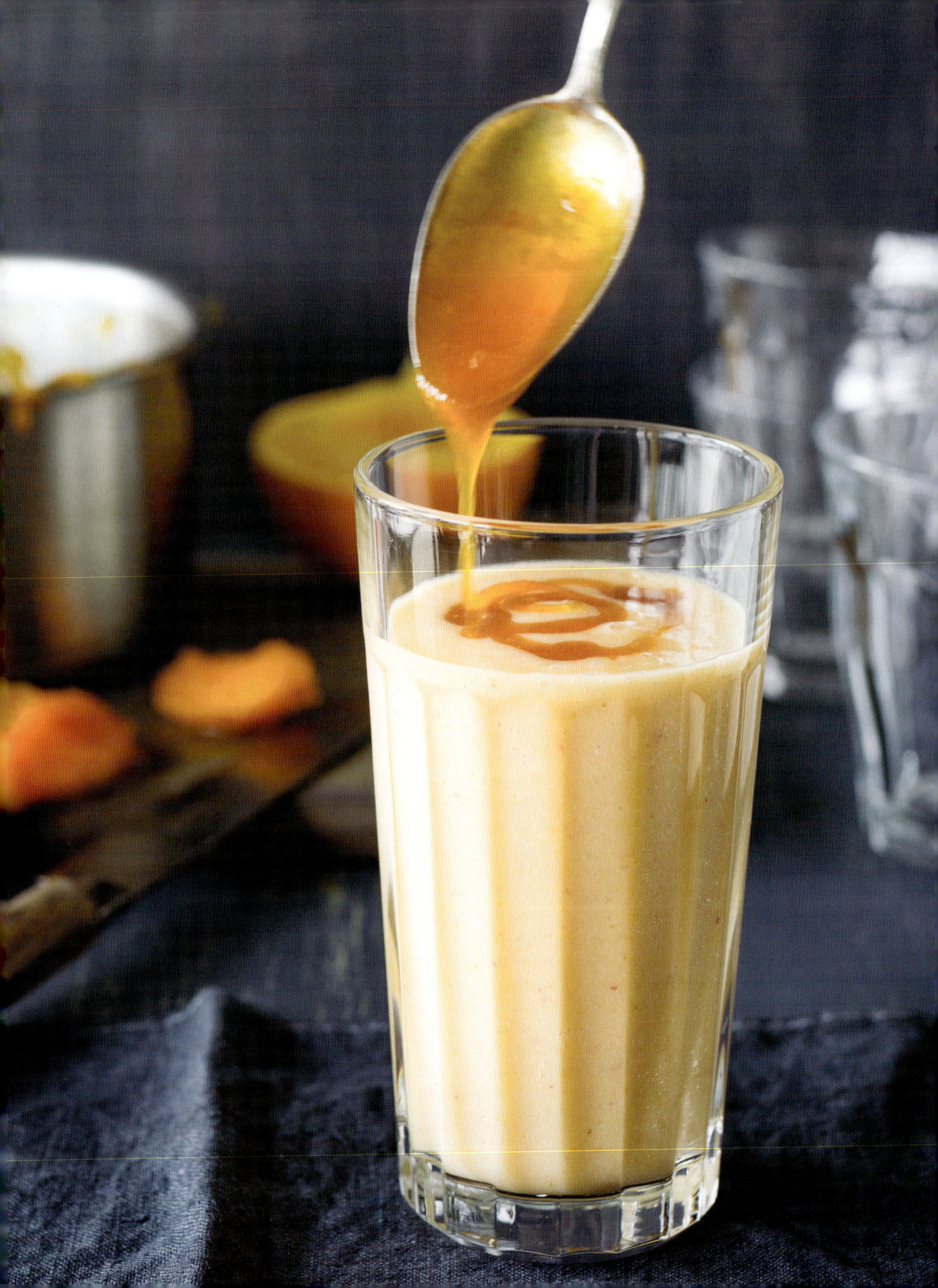

SPICY BUTTERMILK AND MANGO SMOOTHIES

Soothes sore joints

Serves 4
Preparation and cooking 15 minutes + cooling 30 minutes

Ingredients:

4 ripe mangoes, peeled, stoned and chopped
5 cm | 2 in fresh ginger (gingerroot), peeled and finely grated
2 tsp ground turmeric
1 tsp ground cardamom
½ tsp freshly grated nutmeg
½ tsp cayenne (red) pepper
2 tbsp coconut palm sugar
2 ripe bananas
800 ml | 28 fl oz | 3½ cups buttermilk
16 ice cubes

Method:

1. Put the mango in a saucepan with the ginger, turmeric, cardamom, nutmeg, cayenne (red) pepper and coconut palm sugar. Add 100 ml (3⅓ fl oz) of water, then cover and simmer for 6 minutes, stirring occasionally.

2. When the mango is very soft, transfer the mixture to a blender and blend until smooth. Gently pour four heaped dessertspoons to a bowl and set aside. Leave the rest of the mango mixture to cool in the blender.

3. Add the banana, buttermilk and ice cubes to the blender and blend until smooth. Pour the mixture into four large glasses and drizzle the reserved mango purée on top.

BLUEBERRY AND BANANA SMOOTHIES

Helps to lower blood pressure

Serves 2
Preparation 3 minutes

Ingredients:

1 ripe banana, peeled
½ ripe avocado, peeled and stoned
300 ml | 11 fl oz | 1⅓ cups oat milk
150 g | 5 oz | 1 cup frozen blueberries

Method:

1. Put the banana, avocado and oat milk in a blender and blend until smooth.

2. Add the frozen blueberries and blend again. Pour into two bottles or glasses and serve immediately.

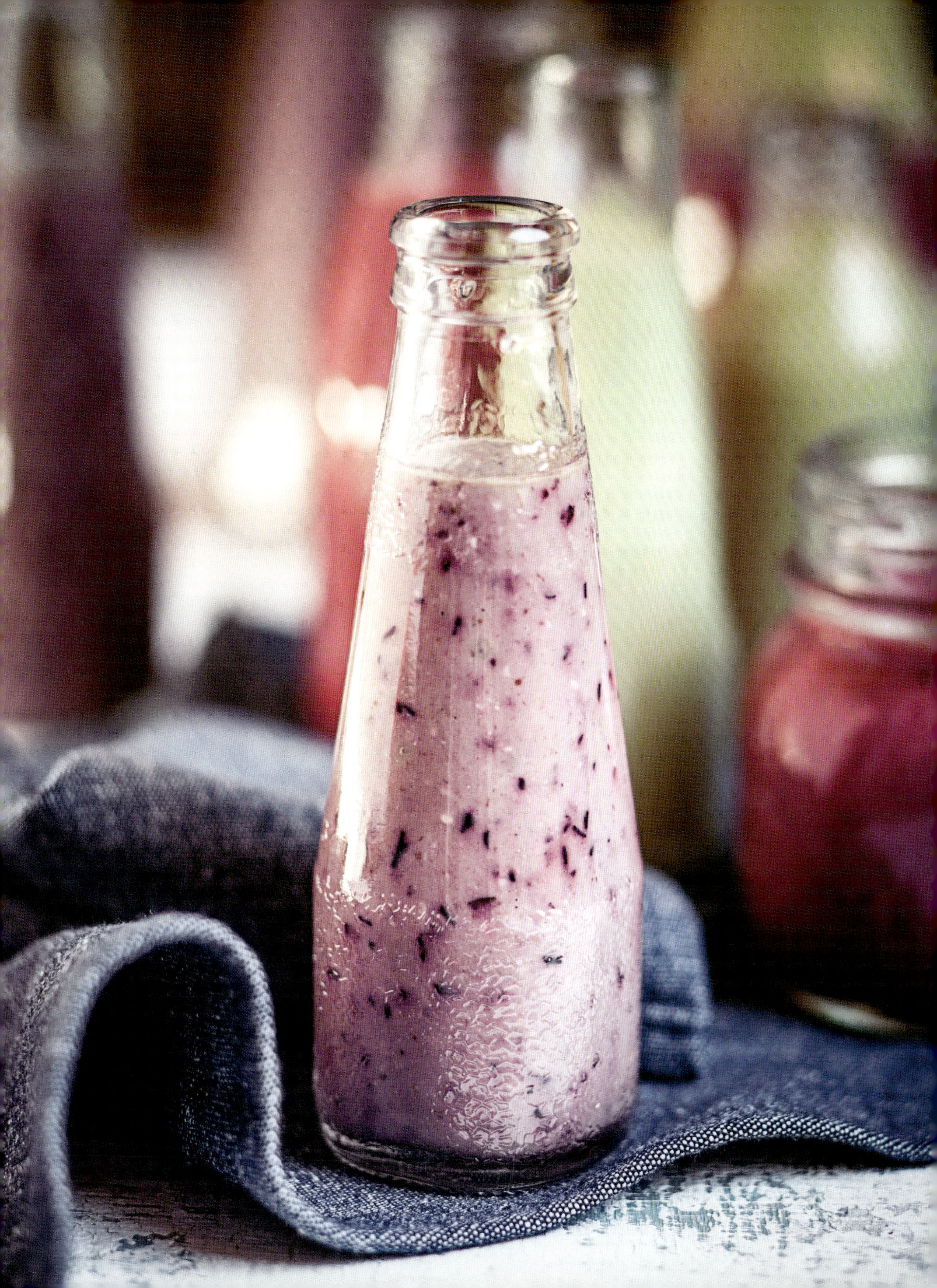

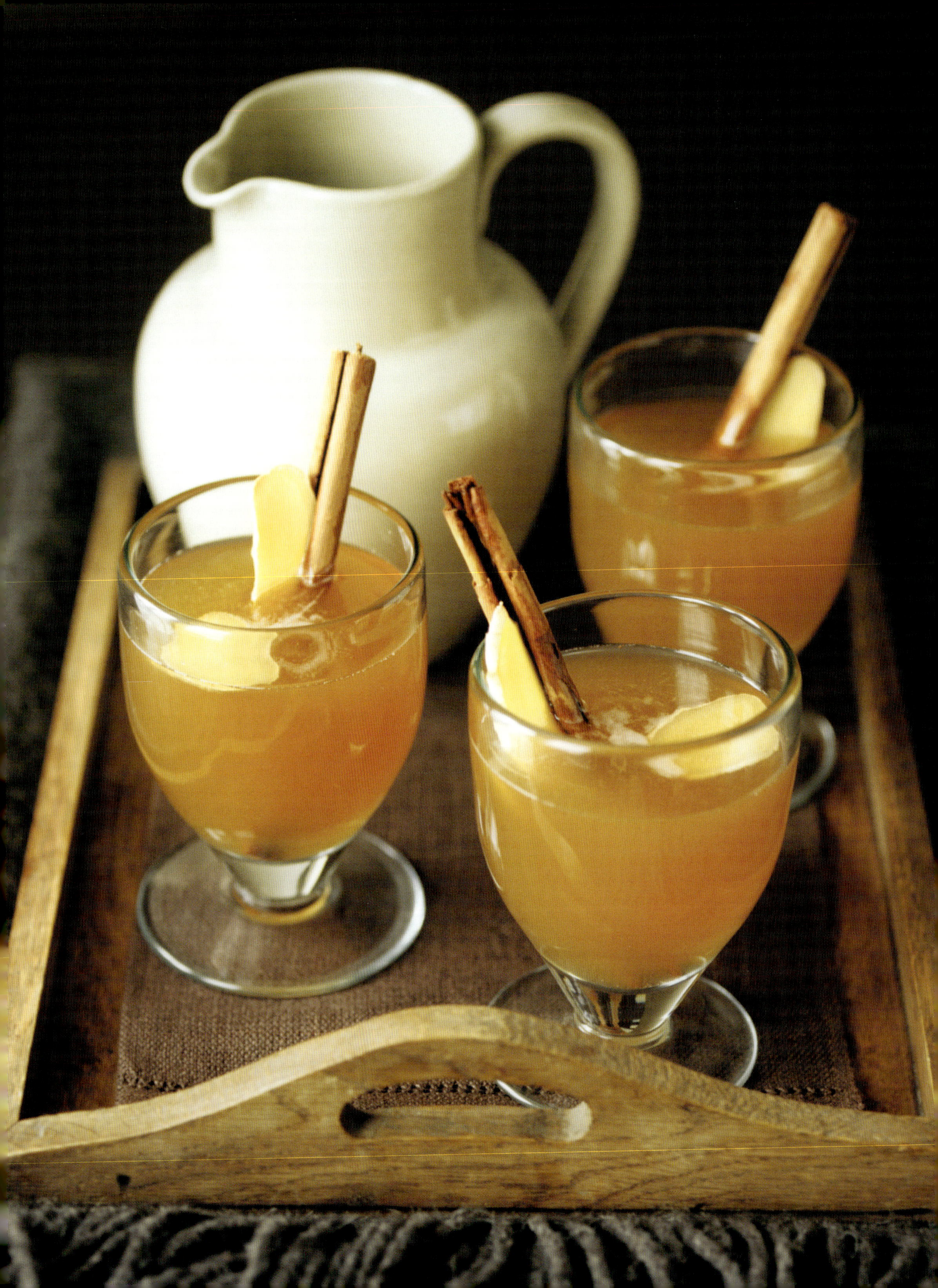

HOT APPLE JUICE WITH CINNAMON AND GINGER

Immune booster

Serves 4
Preparation and cooking 20 minutes

Ingredients:

30 g | 1 oz fresh ginger (gingerroot)
8 medium apples, quartered
4 sticks cinnamon

Method:

1. Cut eight thin slices from the piece of ginger and set aside.

2. Juice the rest of the ginger with the apples and pour into a small saucepan.

3. Add the ginger slices and cinnamon sticks and warm together gently with the lid on for 15 minutes. Ladle into heatproof glasses to serve.

BANANA AND AVOCADO SMOOTHIES

Helps decrease inflammation

Serves 2
Preparation 3 minutes

Ingredients:

1 ripe banana, peeled and chopped
1 ripe avocado, peeled, stoned and chopped
200 ml | 7 fl oz | ⅞ cup oat milk
1 tsp runny honey
1 pinch ground cinnamon
6 ice cubes

Method:

1. Put all of the ingredients in a blender and blend until smooth. Serve immediately.

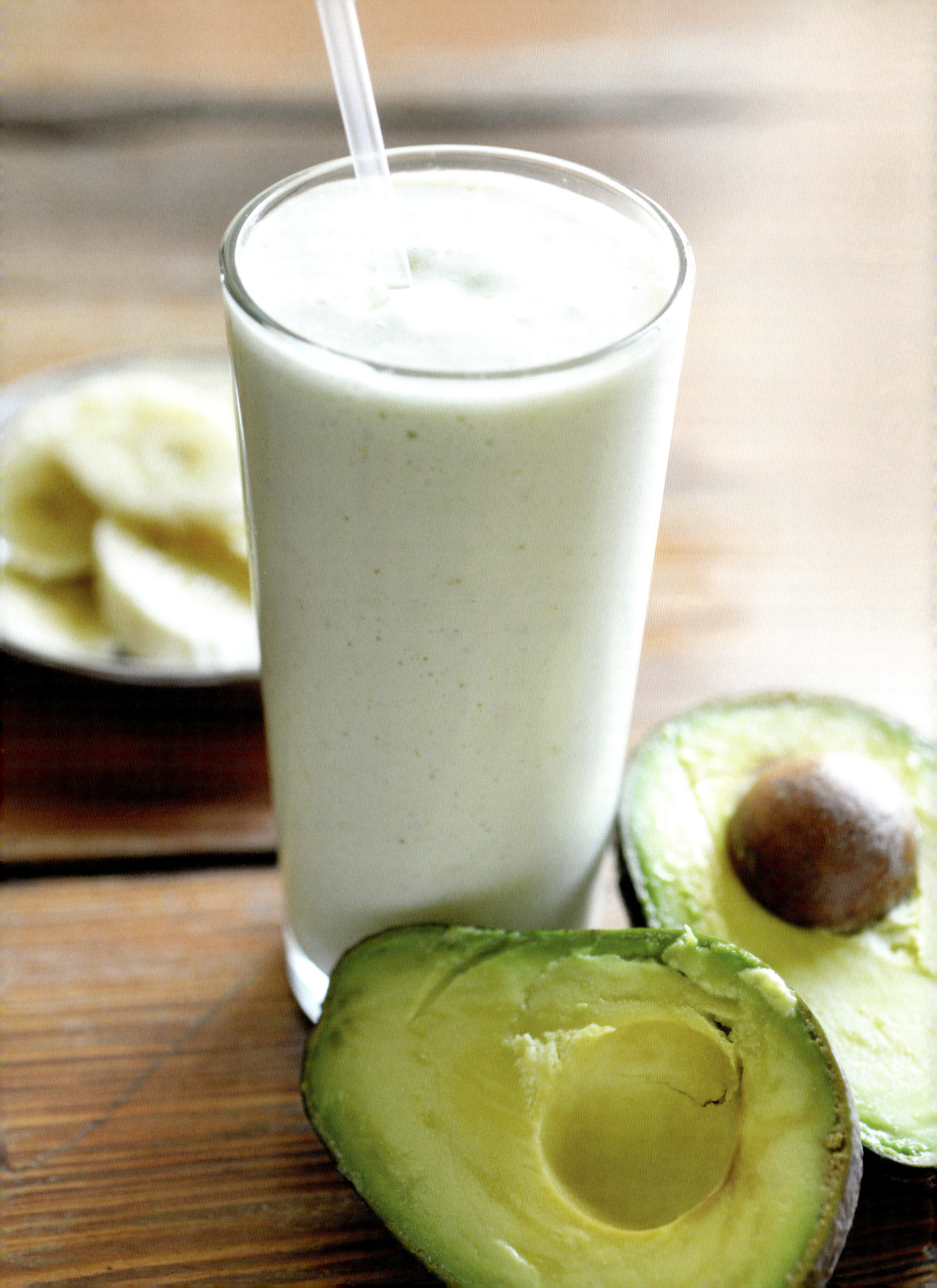

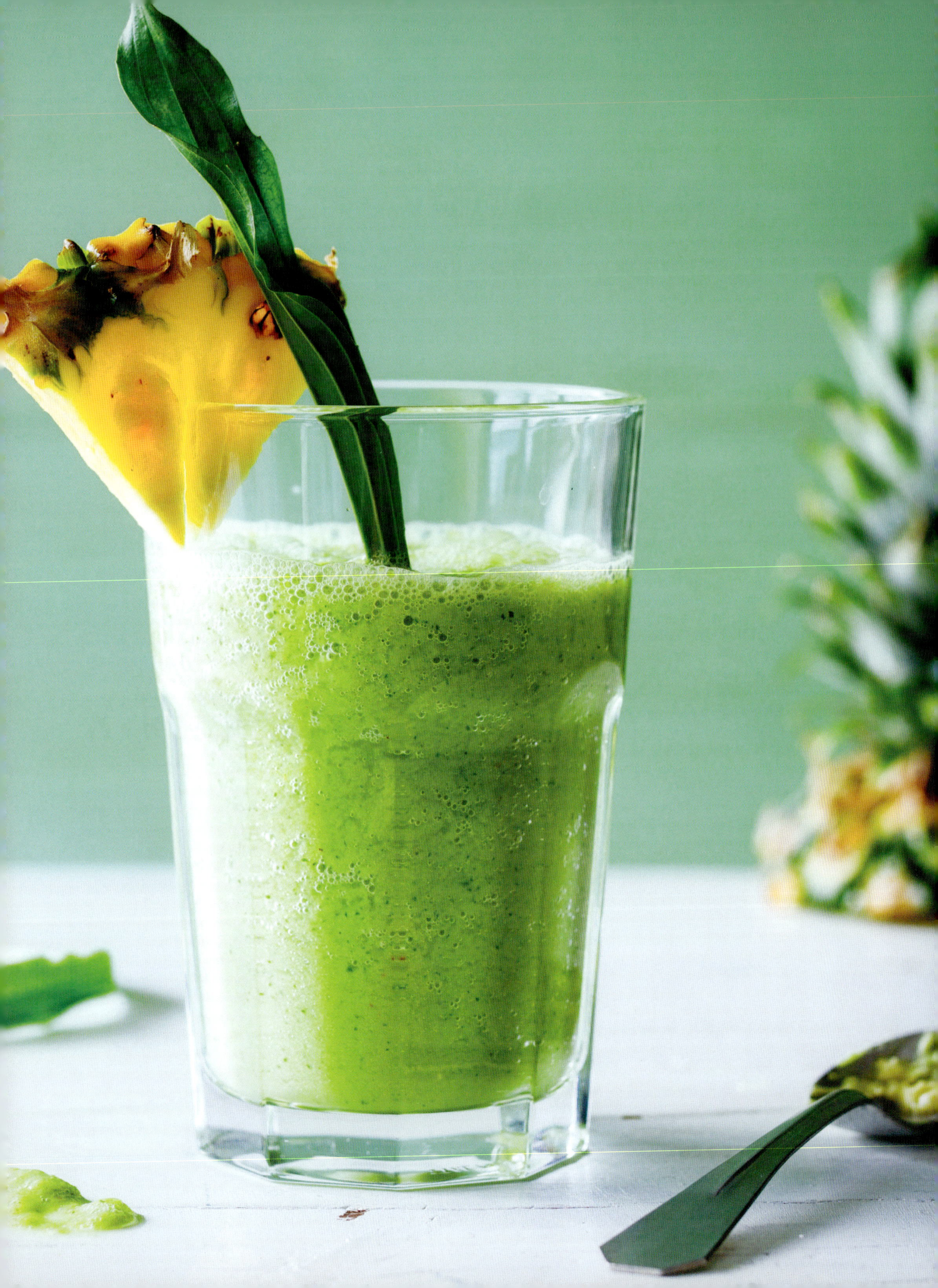

SPRING SMOOTHIES WITH PINEAPPLE AND FRESH HERBS

Cold-killer

Serves 4
Preparation 10 minutes + freezing 2 hours

Ingredients:

6 bananas, peeled and sliced
2 pineapples, leaves removed
30 g | 1 oz | 1 cup kale, stems removed
15 g | ½ oz | ½ cup fresh herbs such as sage or tarragon

Method:

1. Spread out the sliced banana on a lined baking tray (sheet) and freeze for 2 hours or until solid.

2. Cut a thick slice from one of the pineapples, then cut it into quarters and reserve for the garnish. Peel the rest of the pineapples and pass through a juicer to extract the juice.

3. Pour the pineapple juice into a blender and add the kale. Reserve four fresh herb leaves for the garnish, then add the rest to the blender and blend until smooth. Add the frozen banana slices and blend again until smooth, then pour into four glasses and serve immediately, garnished with pineapple wedges and reserved leaves.

EGG AND WHEATGERM SMOOTHIES

Hangover helper

Serves 4
Preparation and cooking 15 minutes

Ingredients:

4 small eggs, separated
4 tbsp honey
800 ml | 28 fl oz | 3½ cups unsweetened almond milk
a pinch salt
4 tbsp wheatgerm
a pinch grated nutmeg
a pinch ground cinnamon

Method:

1. Combine the egg yolks and honey in a mixing bowl and beat with an electric whisk until pale and frothy.

2. Heat the almond milk in a saucepan until bubbles form at the edge. Do not allow the milk to boil.

3. Beat the egg whites with a pinch of salt in a clean, oil-free mixing bowl until stiff.

4. Add the warm milk and wheatgerm to the egg yolk mixture and blend until smooth. Fold into the egg whites and add nutmeg and cinnamon to taste.

5. Pour into glasses and serve immediately.

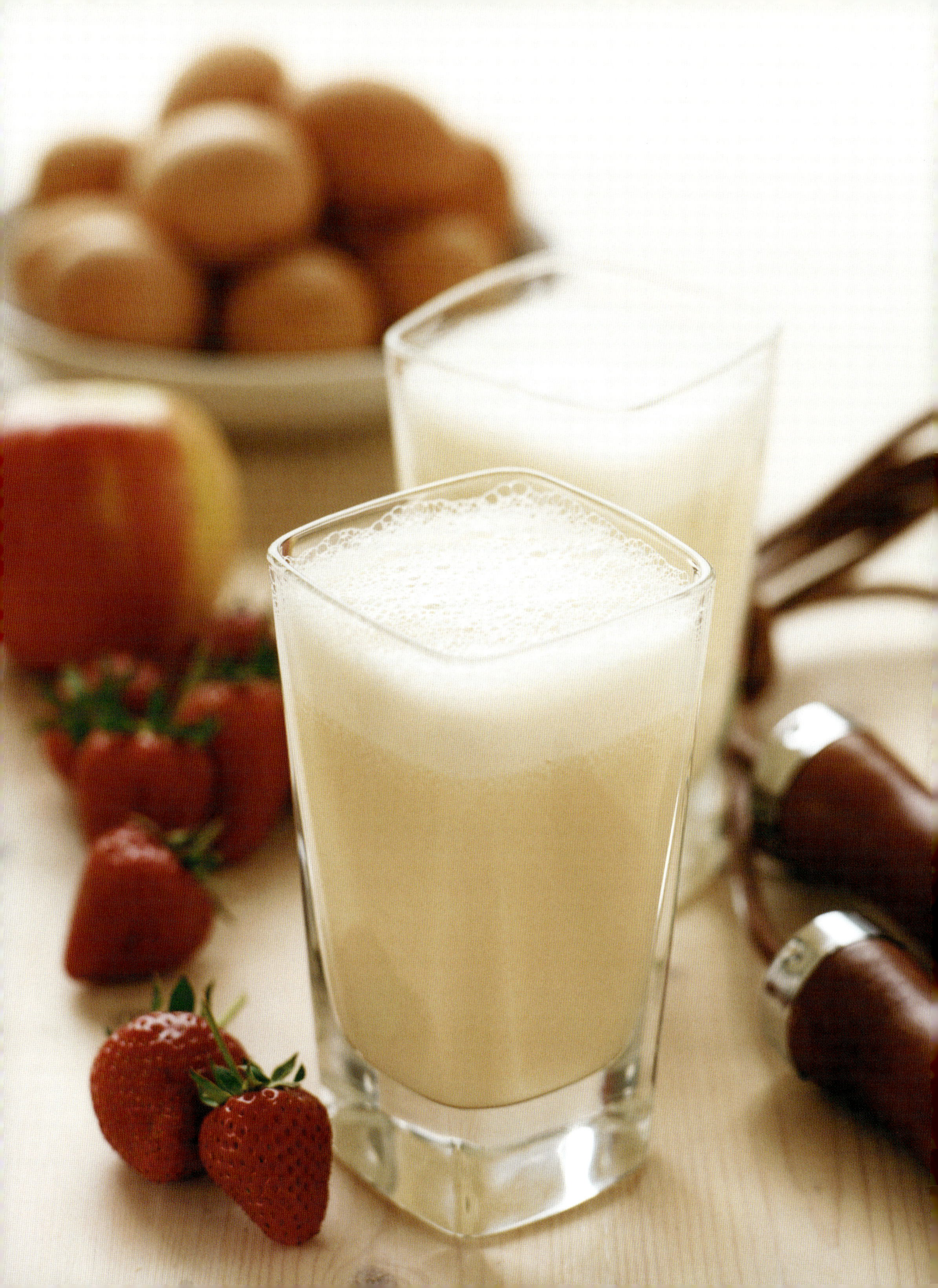

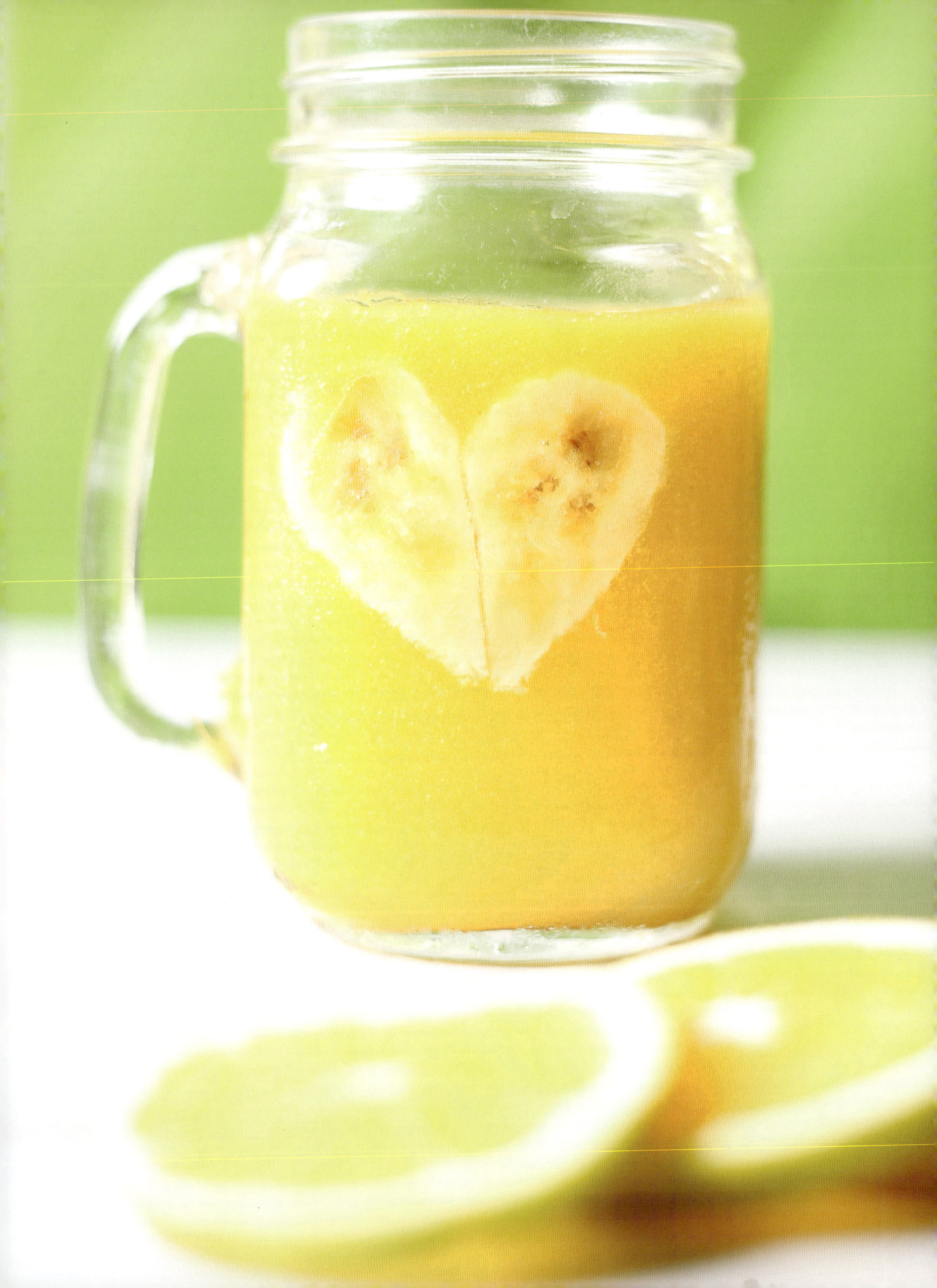

ORANGE AND BANANA JUICE

Stress-buster

Serves 2
Preparation 5 minutes

Ingredients:

2 bananas
4 oranges, peeled
1 lime, peeled, a quarter of the peel reserved

Method:

1. Peel the bananas and retain one of the skins. Cut two diagonal slices from one of the bananas, then cut one side off of each. Press them against the inside of a glass to make a heart shape.

2. Put the reserved banana skin through a juicer with the oranges, lime and the piece of lime peel. Transfer the juice to a blender and blend with the banana until smooth. Pour into the prepared glass and serve immediately.

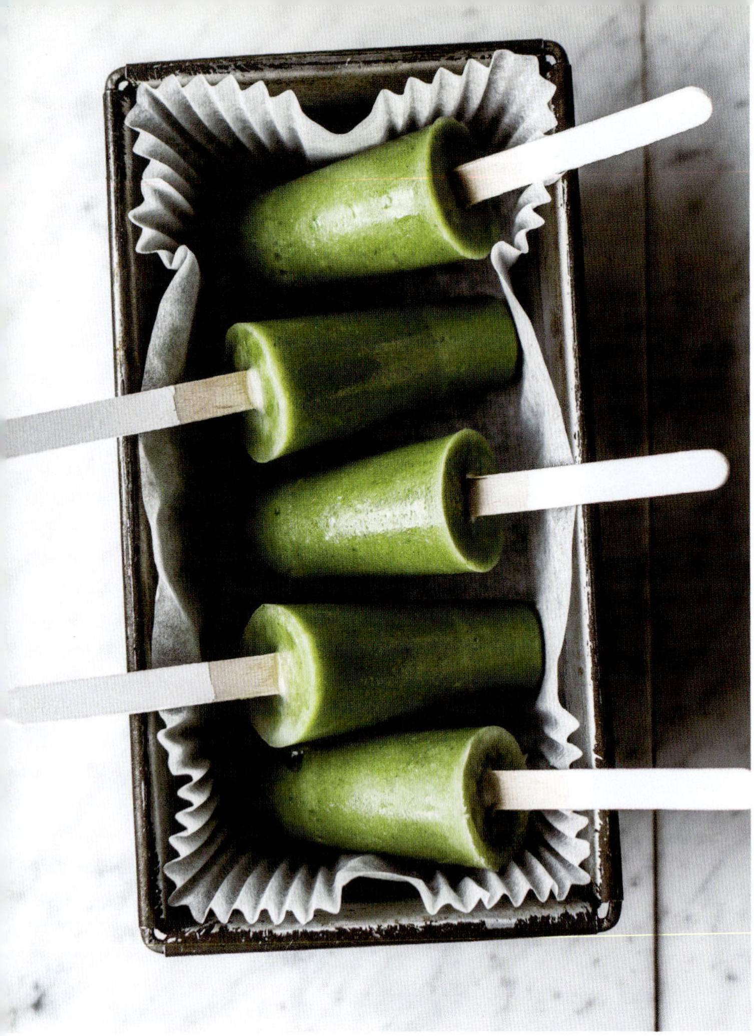
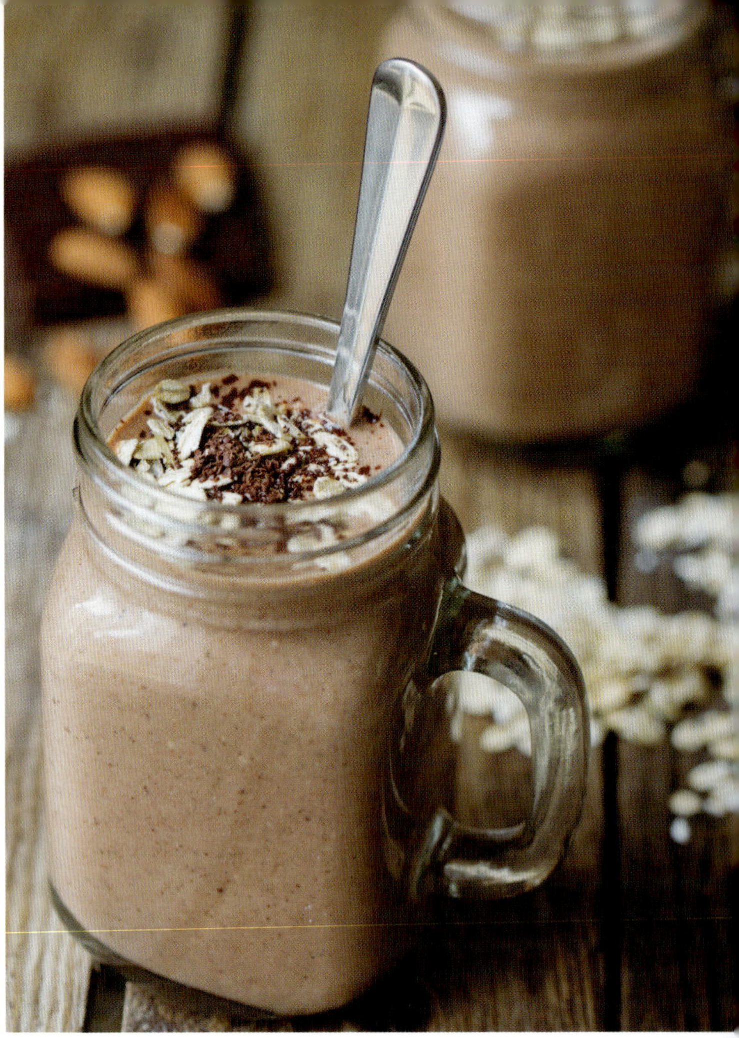
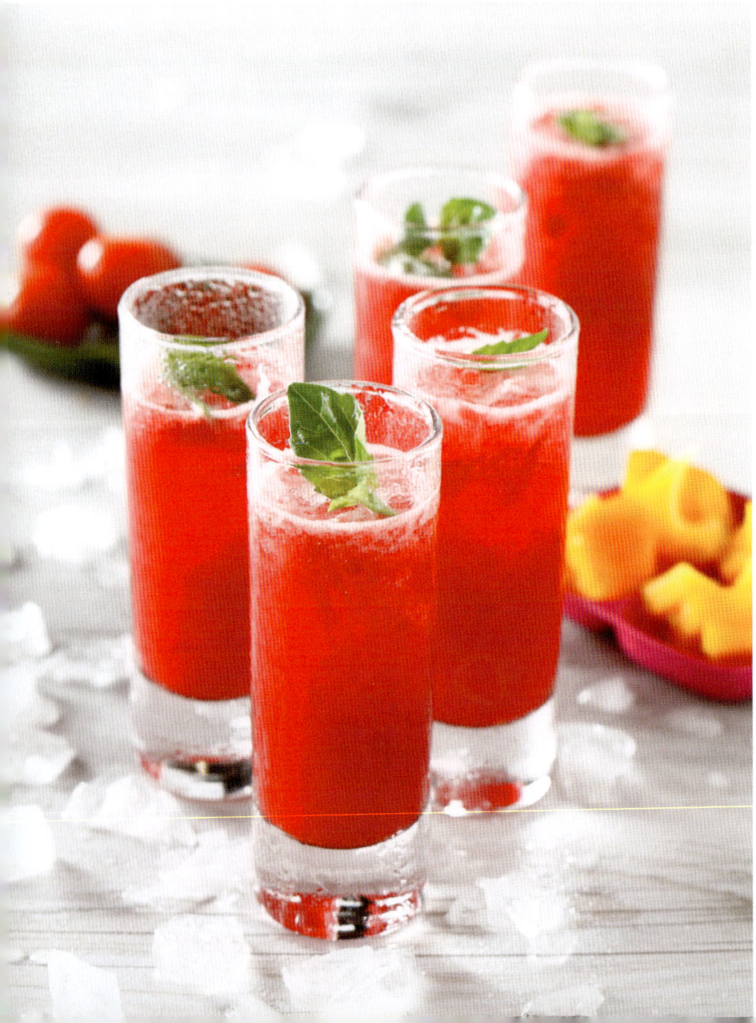
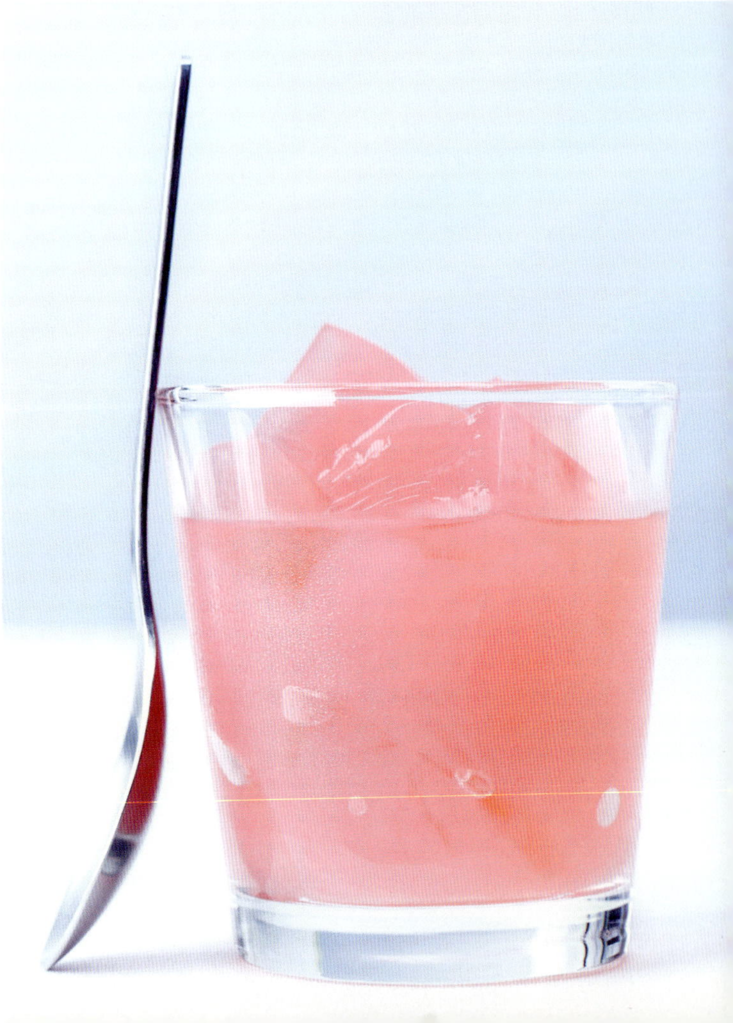

HEALTHY GOURMET

These juices and smoothies make great healthy treats. Indulge in delicacies such as refreshing Viennese Iced Melon Juice, rich Chocolate Superfood Smoothies or tangy Chilled Juice Shots, while still enjoying all the health benefits of the nutritious ingredients.

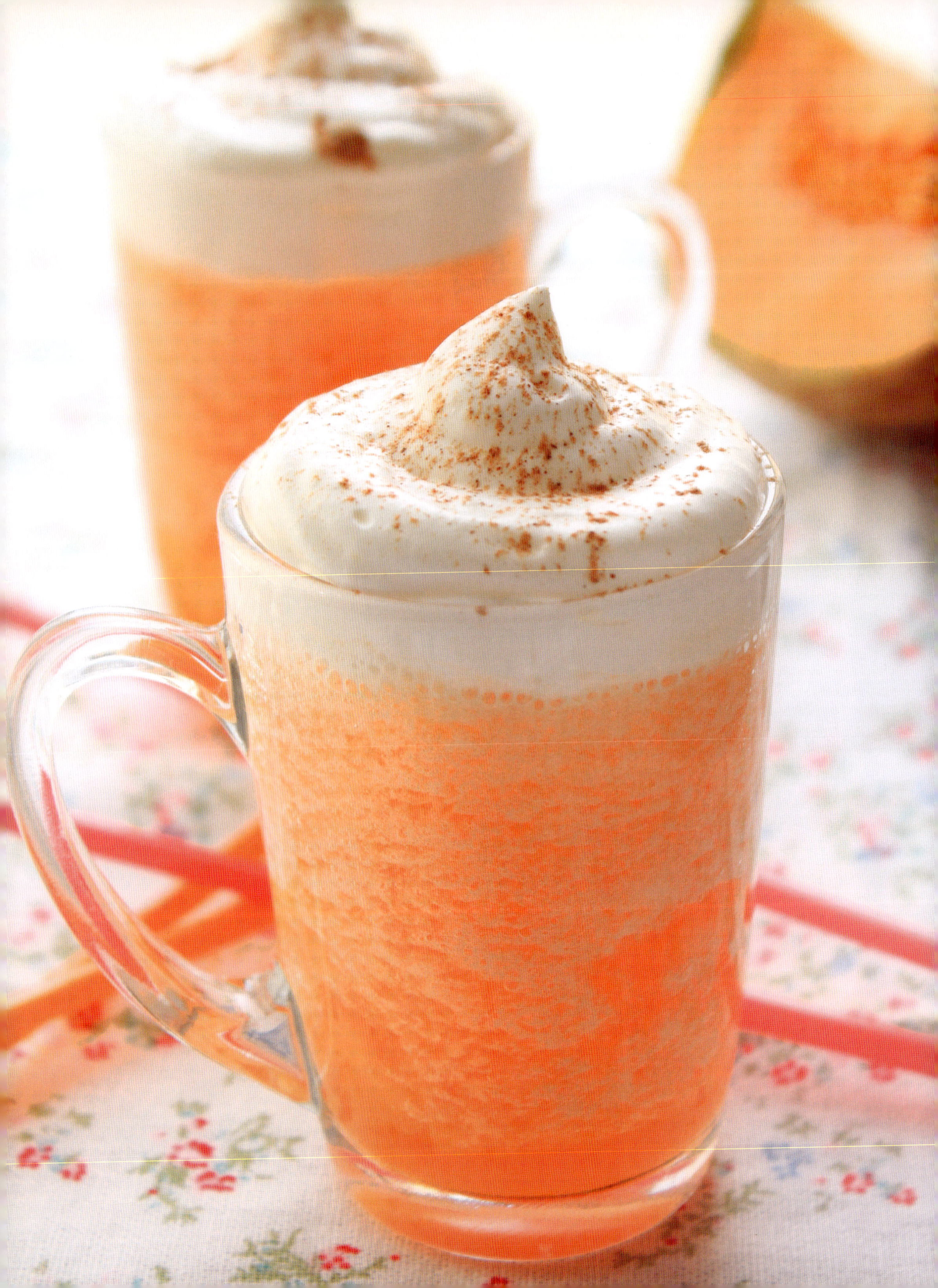

VIENNESE ICED MELON JUICE

Serves 4
Preparation 8 minutes

Ingredients:

320 ml | 11 fl oz | 1⅓ cups canned coconut cream, chilled overnight in a mixing bowl
1 tbsp coconut palm sugar
½ tsp vanilla extract
1 rockmelon (cantaloupe), peeled and seeds removed
600 ml | 21 fl oz | 2½ cups coconut water
16 ice cubes
1 pinch ground cinnamon

Method:

1. Whip the coconut cream, palm sugar and vanilla extract together with an electric whisk until frothy and light.

2. Put the melon, coconut water and ice cubes in a blender and blend until smooth.

3. Divide the smoothie between four glasses and spoon the whipped coconut cream on top. Sprinkle with a little cinnamon and serve immediately.

GREEN SMOOTHIE ICE POPS

Serves 8
Preparation 5 minutes + freezing 4 hours

Ingredients:

65 g | 2¼ oz | 2 cups baby spinach
500 ml | 18 fl oz | 2 cups mango juice
¼ pineapple, peeled, cored and chopped
6 kiwifruits, chopped

Method:

1. Put the spinach and mango juice in a blender and blend until smooth. Add the pineapple and kiwifruit and blend again until smooth.

2. Pour the smoothie into an 8-hole ice pop mould and insert the sticks according to the manufacturer's instructions.

3. Freeze the ice pops for 4 hours or until frozen solid.

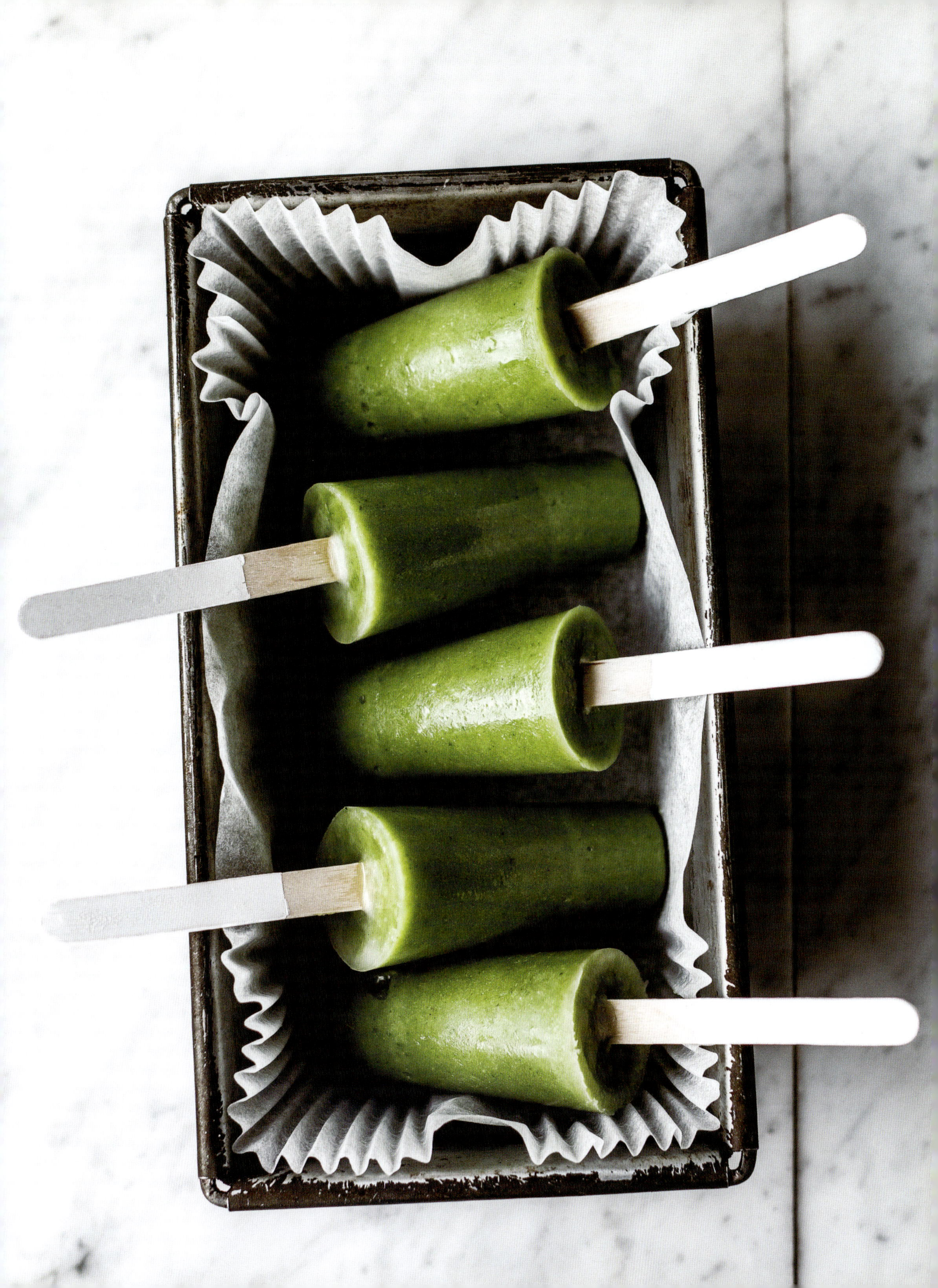

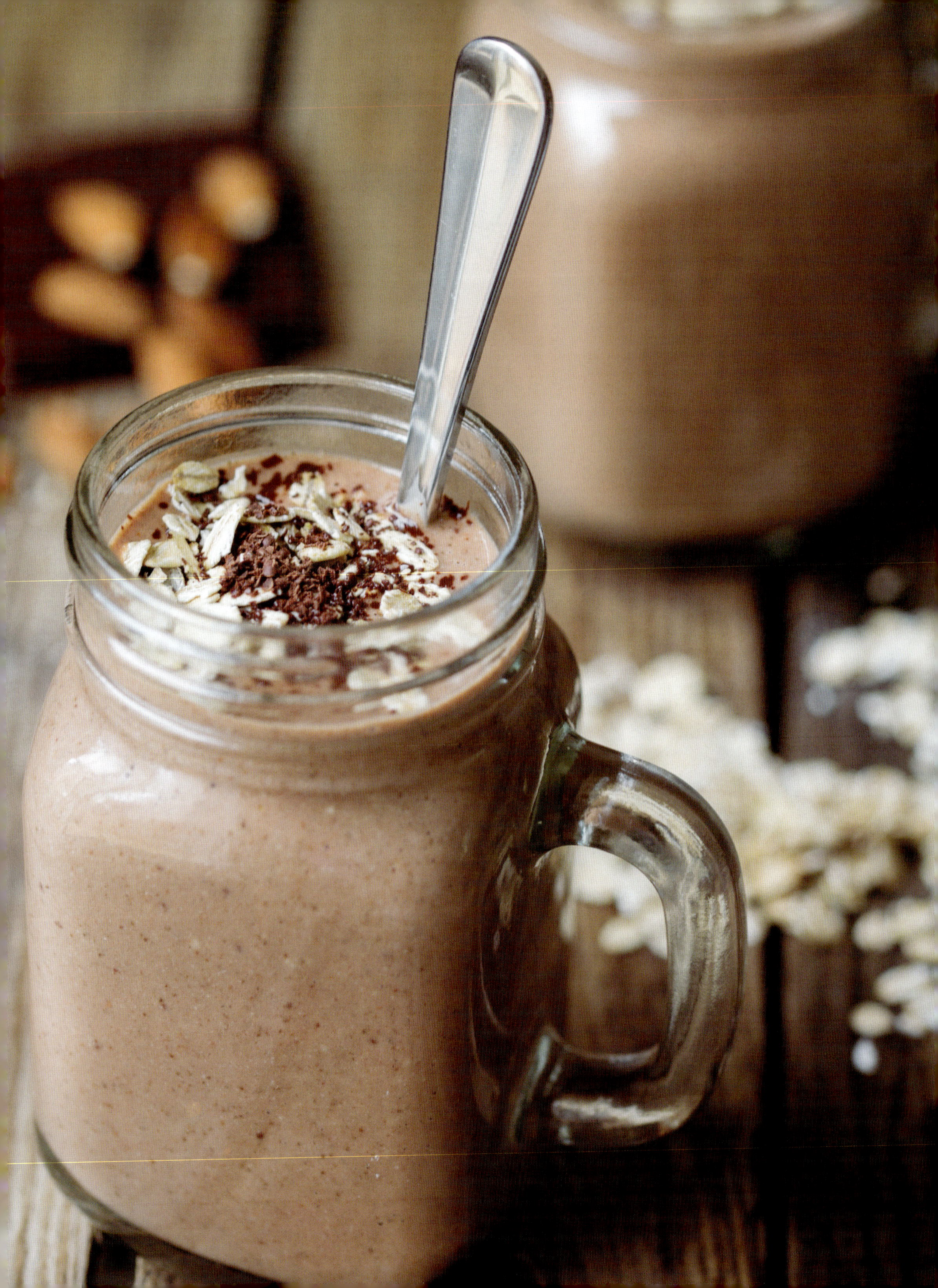

CHOCOLATE SUPERFOOD SMOOTHIES

Serves 4
Preparation 20 minutes

Ingredients:

100 g | 3½ oz | ⅔ cup rolled oats
3 tbsp cocoa powder
400 ml | 14 fl oz | 1⅔ cups chilled coconut milk
500 ml | 18 fl oz | 2 cups almond milk
2 tbsp almond butter
2 tbsp light agave nectar
110 g | 4 oz | ½ cup crushed ice
1 tbsp dark chocolate, grated

Method:

1. Combine most of the oats with the cocoa powder as well as the coconut and almond milk in a food processor or blender. Leave to soak for at least 10 minutes.

2. Add the almond butter and agave nectar. Blend on high for 2 minutes.

3. Add the crushed ice and blend for a further minute until smooth.

4. Pour into glasses and serve with a garnish of the remaining oats and grated chocolate.

Tip: Leave the oats and cocoa powder to soak for as long as you can for a smoother texture.

PEANUT-BUTTER SMOOTHIES

Serves 4
Preparation 3 minutes

Ingredients:

2 ripe bananas, peeled
6 tbsp unsweetened peanut butter
4 tbsp maple syrup
½ tsp ground cinnamon
500 ml | 18 fl oz | 2 cups fat-free frozen yoghurt
400 ml | 14 fl oz | 1⅔ cups almond milk

Method:

1. Put all of the ingredients in a blender and blend until smooth. Divide between four glasses and serve immediately.

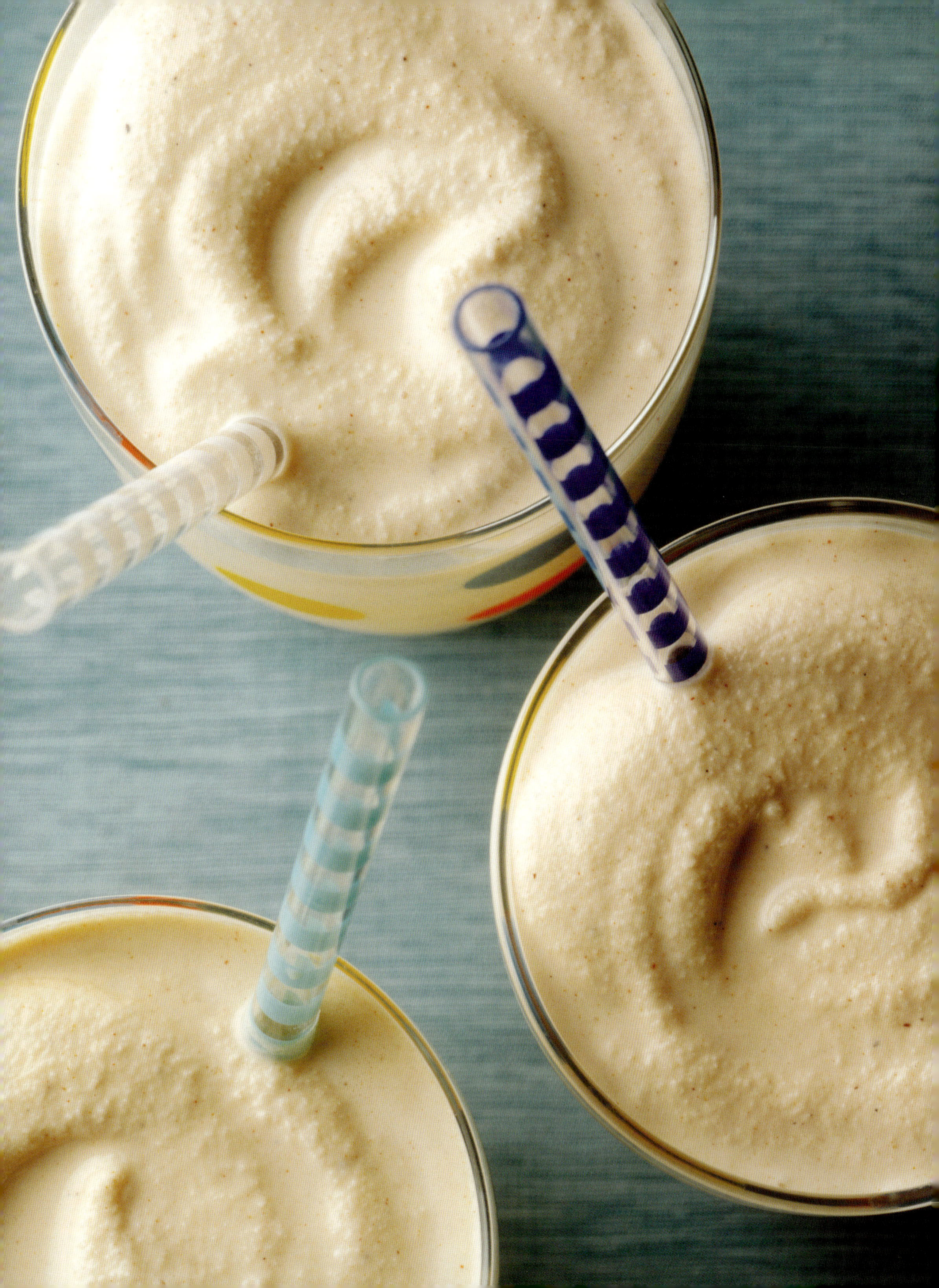

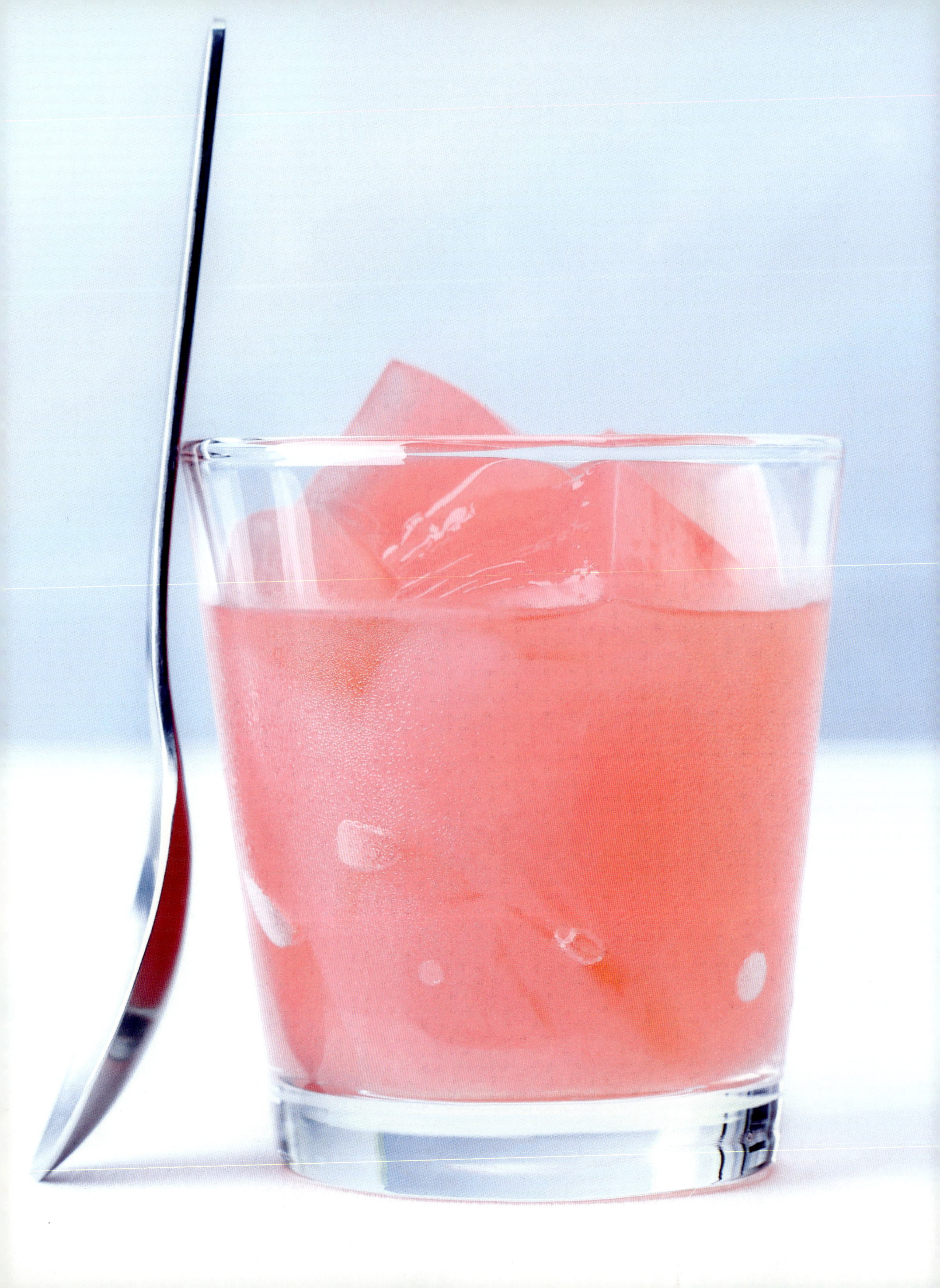

PINK GRAPEFRUIT JUICE WITH AGAR CUBES

Serves 4
Preparation and cooking 10 minutes + chilling 1 hour

Ingredients:

1.75 l | 61 fl oz | 7 cups pink grapefruit juice, freshly squeezed
100 g | 3½ oz | ½ cup white (granulated) sugar
2 sachets agar powder
250 ml | 9 fl oz | 1 cup water

Method:

1. Put 750 ml | 26 fl oz | 3 cups of the grapefruit juice into a pan with the sugar and bring to the boil. Mix the agar powder in water, add to the pan and boil hard for 2 minutes.

2. Pour into a small container, e.g. a gratin dish and leave to cool. Then put into the refrigerator for at least 1 hour.

3. Before serving cut the jelly (jello) into cubes and put into glasses. Top up with the rest of the grapefruit juice and serve.

STRAWBERRY CAPPUCCINOS

Serves 2
Preparation 10 minutes

Ingredients:

200 g | 7 oz | 1⅓ cups strawberries, hulled
200 g | 7 oz | 1⅓ cups raspberries
450 g | 16 oz | 3 cups seedless watermelon, peeled and diced
1 tbsp mint, chopped, plus 2 sprigs to garnish
150 ml | 5 fl oz | ⅔ cup skimmed milk

Method:

1. Ensure all of the ingredients are well chilled before starting.

2. Pass the strawberries, raspberries, watermelon and mint through a juicer to extract the juice, then divide between two glasses.

3. Use a milk frother to turn the milk into a foam. Alternatively, pour the milk into a mixing bowl and use an electric whisk on high speed to froth the milk. Spoon the foam on top of the juice and garnish with mint. Serve immediately.

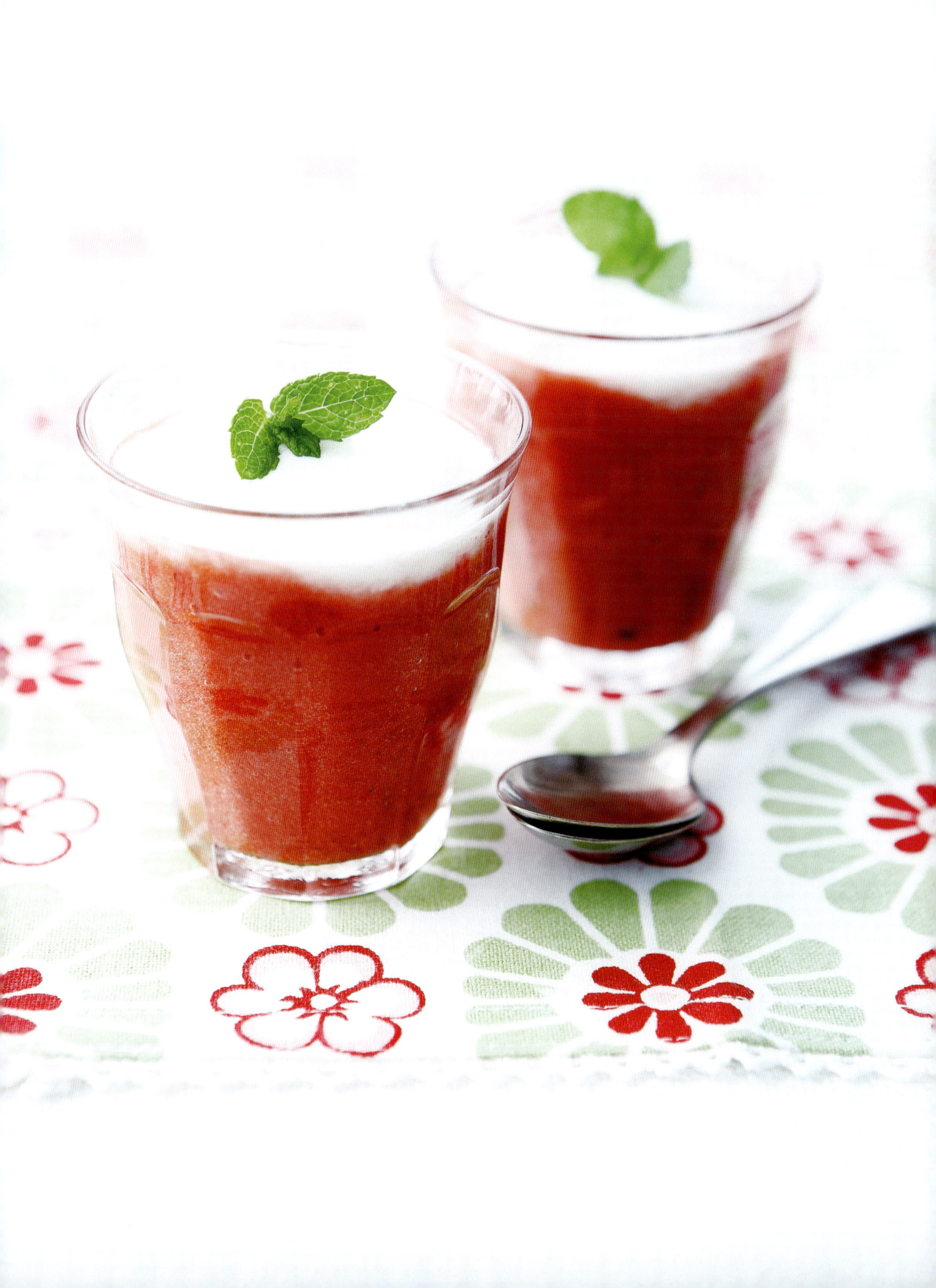

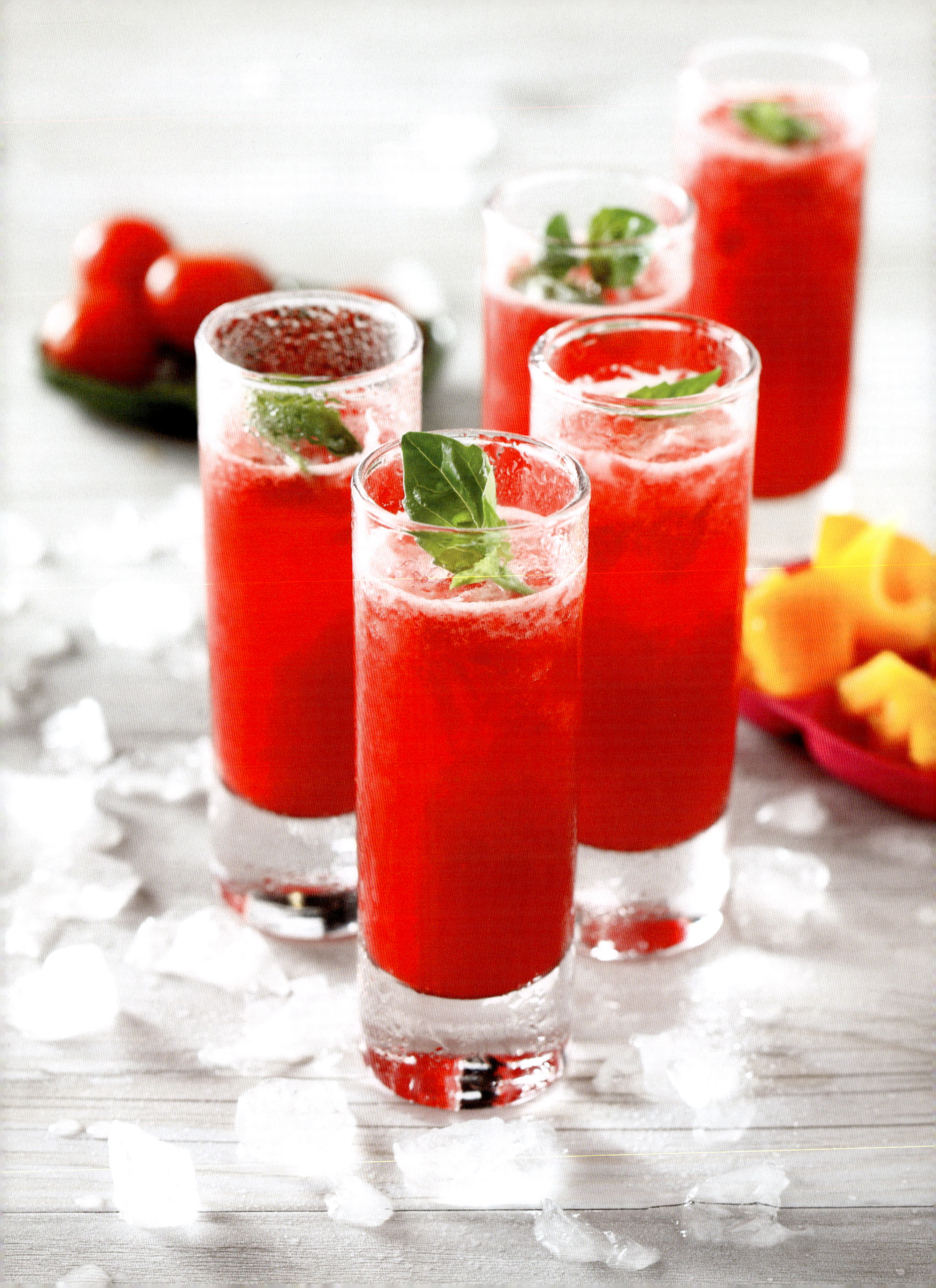

CHILLED JUICE SHOTS

Serves 6
Preparation 4 minutes

Ingredients:

10 cherry tomatoes
150 g | 5 oz | 1 cup raspberries
1 yellow capsicum (pepper), quartered, seeds and stalk removed
2 red delicious apples, quartered
12 leaves basil

Method:

1. Pass the tomatoes, raspberries, capsicum (pepper), apples and six of the basil leaves through a juicer.

2. Divide the juice between six frozen shot glasses and garnish each one with a basil leaf.

WEIGHTS AND MEASURES

Weights and measures differ from country to country, but with these handy conversion charts cooking has never been easier!

Cup Measurements

One cup of these commonly used ingredients is equal to the following weights.

Ingredient	Metric	Imperial
Apples (dried and chopped)	125 g	4½ oz
Apricots (dried and chopped)	190 g	6¾ oz
Berries (frozen)	150 g	5 oz
Coconut (desiccated/fine)	90 g	3 oz
Crushed ice	250 g	9 oz
Fruit (dried)	170 g	6 oz
Golden syrup (dark cane sugar syrup)	315 g	11 oz
Honey	315 g	11 oz
Leafy greens (spinach, kale, watercress)	35 g	1¼ oz
Nuts (chopped)	115 g	4 oz
Rolled oats	100 g	3⅓ oz
Strawberries (fresh)	200 g	7 oz
Sugar (granulated)	225 g	8 oz
Yoghurt	150 g	5 oz

Oven Temperatures

Celsius	Fahrenheit	Gas mark
120	250	1
150	300	2
160	320	3
180	350	4
190	375	5
200	400	6
220	430	7
230	450	8
250	480	9

Liquid Measures

Cup	Metric	Imperial
¼ cup	63 ml	2¼ fl oz
½ cup	125 ml	4½ fl oz
¾ cup	188 ml	6⅔ fl oz
1 cup	250 ml	8¾ fl oz
1¾ cup	438 ml	15½ fl oz
2 cups	500 ml	17½ fl oz
4 cups	1 litre	35 fl oz

Spoon	Metric	Imperial
¼ teaspoon	1.25 ml	1/25 fl oz
½ teaspoon	2.5 ml	1/12 fl oz
1 teaspoon	5 ml	⅙ fl oz
1 tablespoon	15 ml	½ fl oz

Weight Measures

Metric	Imperial
10 g	¼ oz
15 g	½ oz
20 g	¾ oz
30 g	1 oz
60 g	2 oz
115 g	4 oz (¼ lb)
125 g	4½ oz
145 g	5 oz
170 g	6 oz
185 g	6½ oz
200 g	7 oz
225 g	8 oz (½ lb)
300 g	10½ oz
330 g	11½ oz
370 g	13 oz
400 g	14 oz
425 g	15 oz
455 g	16 oz (1 lb)
500 g	17½ oz (1 lb 1½ oz)
600 g	21 oz (1 lb 5 oz)
650 g	23 oz (1 lb 7 oz)
750 g	26½ oz (1 lb 10½ oz)
1000 g (1 kg)	35 oz (2 lb 3 oz)

INDEX

Apple, Celery and Black Radish Juice	14	Orange and Aloe Juice	50
Banana and Avocado Smoothies	70	Orange and Banana Juice	77
Berry Smoothies	9	Peanut-Butter Smoothies	86
Blackberry and Raspberry Smoothies	13	Pear, Apricot and Carrot Juice	38
Black Kale and Wild Garlic Smoothies	29	Pink Grapefruit Juice with Agar Cubes	89
Blueberry and Banana Smoothies	66	Purple Carrot and Strawberry Smoothies	26
Chilled Juice Shots	93	Ruby Juice	33
Chocolate Superfood Smoothies	85	Spicy Buttermilk and Mango Smoothies	65
Egg and Wheatgerm Smoothies	74	Spinach and Pear Smoothies with Chia Seeds	21
Energising Juice	46	Spring Smoothies with Pineapple and Fresh Herbs	73
Fig and Walnut Smoothies	57	Strawberry and Almond Smoothies	54
Fitness Smoothies with Oat Bran	49	Strawberry and Coconut Smoothies with Goji Berries	10
Fresh Apple and Celery Juice	41	Strawberry and Melon Antioxidant Juice	17
Green Smoothie Ice Pops	82	Strawberry Cappuccinos	90
Green Smoothies with Blueberries and Wheatgrass	37	Vegetable Juice	62
Hot Apple Juice with Cinnamon and Ginger	69	Viennese Iced Melon Juice	81
Kumquat and Pineapple Juice	18	Vitamin-Rich Juice	22
Layered Juice with Agave and Coconut	34	Watercress Cocktail with Melon and Pears	53
Mandarin and Passionfruit Smoothies	58	Watermelon and Strawberry Refreshing Juice	30
Muesli and Apple Smoothies	45		